Penguin Education
Penguin English Project Stage Three

Identity
Edited by Myra Barrs

Identity
Edited by Myra Barrs

Society
Edited by Myra Barrs

Things
Edited by Tony Burgess

Bonds
Edited by Pat D'Arcy

Out of this World
Edited by Peter Griffiths

The Modern Experience
Edited by Noel Hardy

Penguin English Projec

Edited by Myra Barrs

Stage Three **Identity**

Penguin Education

Penguin Education,
A Division of Penguin Books Ltd,
Harmondsworth, Middlesex, England
Penguin Books Australia Ltd,
Ringwood, Victoria, Australia

First published 1973

Designed by Ivan Atanasoff
Set in Garamond by
Oliver Burridge Filmsetting Ltd,
Crawley, Sussex
Made and printed in Great Britain
by C. Tinling & Co. Ltd,
Prescot and London

Contents

A Hot Bath

The mirror over my bureau seemed slightly warped and much too silver. The face in it looked like the reflection in a ball of dentist's mercury. I thought of crawling in between the bedsheets and trying to sleep, but that appealed to me about as much as stuffing a dirty, scrawled-over letter into a fresh, clean envelope. I decided to take a hot bath.

There must be quite a few things a hot bath won't cure, but I don't know many of them. Whenever I'm sad I'm going to die, or so nervous I can't sleep, or in love with somebody I won't be seeing for a week, I slump down just so far and then I say: 'I'll go take a hot bath.'

I meditate in the bath. The water needs to be very hot, so hot you can barely stand putting your foot in it. Then you lower yourself, inch by inch, till the water's up to your neck.

I remember the ceilings over every bathtub I've stretched out in. I remember the texture of the ceilings and the cracks and the colours and the damp spots and the light fixtures. I remember the tubs, too: the antique griffin-legged tubs, and the modern coffin-shaped tubs, and the fancy pink marble tubs overlooking indoor lily ponds, and I remember the shapes and sizes of the water taps and the different sorts of soap-holders.

I never feel so much myself as when I'm in a hot bath.

I lay in that tub on the seventeenth floor of this hotel for-women-only, high up over the jazz and push of New York, for near on to an hour, and I felt myself growing pure again. I don't believe in baptism or the waters of Jordan or anything like that, but I guess I feel about a hot bath the way those religious people feel about holy water.

I said to myself: 'Doreen is dissolving, Lenny Shepherd is dissolving, Frankie is dissolving, New York is dissolving, they are all dissolving away and none of them matter any more. I don't know them, I have never known them and I am very pure. All that liquor and those sticky kisses I saw and the dirt that settled on my skin on the way back is turning into something pure.'

The longer I lay there in the clear hot water the purer I felt, and when I stepped out at last and wrapped myself in one of the big, soft, white, hotel bath-towels I felt pure and sweet as a new baby.

Sylvia Plath *The Bell Jar*

Stripping Walls

I have been practical as paint today,
wholesome as bread –
I have stripped walls. I rose early and felt
clean-limbed
And steady-eyed and said 'Today I will strip
those walls.'
I have not been chewing my nails and gazing
through windows
And grovelling for a subject or happiness.
There was the subject,
Simple and tall. And when the baker called he
was civil
And looking at me with some respect he said
'I see you're stripping walls' – I could see he
liked me.
And when I opened the door to the
greengrocer, I glinted my eyes
And leaned nonchalantly and poked some
tomatoes and said as an aside
'I'm stripping walls today.' 'Are you?' he
asked, interested, and I said
'Yes, just stripping those walls.' I could feel
my forearms thicken, grow
Hairy, and when the laundry arrived I met it
with rolled sleeves.
'Stripping walls?' he asked. 'Yeah,' I said, as
if it were unimportant,
'Stripping walls. You know.' He nodded and
smiled as if he knew.
And with a step like a spring before the meal
I strode
Down to the pub and leaned and sipped ale
and heard them talk
How one had cleared land that morning,
another chopped wood.
When an eye caught mine I winked and
flipped my head. 'I've been
Stripping walls,' I said. 'Have you?' 'Yeah,
you know, just stripping.'
They nodded. 'Can be tricky,' one mumbled.
I nodded. 'It can be that.'
'Plaster,' another said. 'Holes,' I said.
'Workmanship,' said another
And shook his head. 'Yeah, have a drink,'
I said.
And I whistled through the afternoon, and
stood once or twice
At the door-jamb, the stripper dangling from
my fingers.
'Stripping?' asked passing neighbours,
I nodded and they went on happy
They were happy that I was stripping walls.
It meant a lot.

When it grew dark, I went out for the
freshness. 'Hey!' I called up,
'I've been stripping walls!' 'Just fancy that!'
answered the moon with
A long pale face like Hopkins. 'Hey, fellers!'
he called to the stars,
'This little hairy runt has been stripping
walls!' 'Bully for him,' chimed
The Pole star, remote and cool as Virgil,
'he's a good, good lad.'
I crept to the kitchen, pursued by celestial
laughter.
'You've done well today,' she said. 'Shall we
paint tomorrow?'
'Ah, shut up!' I said, and started hacking my
nails.

Brian Jones

Self and Not-Self

We must now endeavour to paint a picture of life as it probably appears from the infant's point of view. This must of course be largely a matter of guess-work, since memories – even if recalled under deep analysis or hypnosis – must be influenced by the adult medium through which they are expressed. However, we do know something of the conditions which limit the infant's appreciation of its surroundings. For example it is unable to use its eyes together – to fixate – in such a way as to get stereoscopic vision with a sense of depth and distance. Further, lacking the experience of reaching for things and of locomotion, it cannot, to begin with, have any idea of space, and this will for a time retard the building up of an orderly mental picture of the rooms, passages, etc., in which it has been. For the infant, therefore, people will not 'come and go', they will 'appear and disappear' as for us they still do in dreams and in supernatural fantasies.

People themselves have not in the infant's eyes the distinctive features which for us constitute their personalities; though certainly it is probable that the infant is instinctively attracted to the mother by smell. Language, too, is meaningless for the infant except for tone-modulation and rhythm, which probably evoke emotional responses just as smell evokes appetites from the beginning. . . .

From the known conditions of infant life then, we can infer with great probability that the infant, to begin with, cannot appreciate the distinction between itself and its mother. It *discovers* its body by degrees, realizing that in some way an impulse to move is accompanied by felt or seen movement; in other words the wish and the act are experienced as one. *By contrast with the self it must gradually distinguish the 'not-self'* which restricts its movements and acts in a way not expected or wished by itself. The self makes its first appearance, as it were, as docile but rather helpless; the not-self emerges as powerful for pleasure or for displeasure, and by this last possibility it stands out as an inharmonious part of experience. Sometimes it conforms to wish and gratifies need; sometimes the agency, now perceived as external, acts in disagreeable or unanticipated ways. The very birth of self-consciousness then, for the helpless infant, must be attended by experience of wish and frustration, by gratifications, longings, and by *anxiety*, rising at times to angry instinctive cries and struggles directed at the newly discovered 'others'.

Ian D. Suttie *The Origins of Love and Hate*

Once upon a time

Once upon a time and a very good time it was there was a moocow coming down along the road and this moocow that was coming down along the road met a nicens little boy named baby tuckoo. . . .

His father told him that story: his father looked at him through a glass: he had a hairy face.

He was baby tuckoo. The moocow came down the road where Betty Byrne lived: she sold lemon platt.

O, the wild rose blossoms
On the little green place.

He sang that song. That was his song.

O, the green wothe
botheth.

When you wet the bed first it is warm then it gets cold. His mother put on the oilsheet. That had the queer smell.

His mother had a nicer smell than his father. She played on the piano the sailor's hornpipe for him to dance. He danced:

Tralala lala
Tralala tralaladdy,
Tralala lala
Tralala lala.

Uncle Charles and Dante clapped. They were older than his father and mother but uncle Charles was older than Dante.

Dante had two brushes in her press. The brush with the maroon velvet back was for Michael Davitt and the brush with the green velvet back was for Parnell. Dante gave him a cachou every time he brought her a piece of tissue paper.

The Vances lived in number seven. They had a different father and mother. They were Eileen's father and mother. When they were grown up he was going to marry Eileen. He hid under the table. His mother said: 'O, Stephen will apologize.'

Dante said: 'O, if not, the eagles will come and pull out his eyes.'

Pull out his eyes,
Apologize,
Apologize,
Pull out his eyes.

Apologize,
Pull out his eyes,
Pull out his eyes,
Apologize.

James Joyce
Portrait of the Artist as a Young Man

He has a veranda with a view

He has a veranda with a view.

The view is unpeopled. It is his, and not a place for people to mar. It cannot be prised apart from his first rainbow, his first skyscape, first clouds and stars and sunshine showers and whirlwinds. It is eternally silent.

Nearer, at his foot, below the veranda, under the plane-trees, the footpath and the roadway do give up, from time to time, the sound of strange bright footsteps, of wheels stopping and starting, of the road-sweeper's shovel as it scrapes under the horsemanure, of the gipsy cries tearing at the throats of the fish-oh, the rabbit-oh, the tinker, the vendor of pegs and clothes-props. He hears whistlers come nearer and fade to nothing to make place for the next whistler and the next. Once he hears a barrel-organ. Once he hears a man singing nearer and nearer and then farther and farther, singing the same words over and over again so that he learns them:

'When the moon shines tonight on Charlie Chaplin,
His boots are crackin',
From want of blackin',
And his trousers will need a little mendin'
Before they send him
To the Dardanelles.'

Behind his back, in the house, Mother sings, at the same time and in the same tune:

'When the moon shines tonight on pretty Red Wing. . . .'

In autumn, when the bluestone street-drain is flooded with leaves, he sees, he hears, big pinafored girls, whose schoolbags ride their shoulder-blades, wading the rustles of leaves, and squealing falsely (he recognizes the falsity) or, floppy hats inclined inwards to each other, whispering secretively as tiger-lilies. At twilight, the lamplighter is known to be moving, never near, always far off, at one or other end of the street, unseen with his unseen wand that pins staid large stars into the street-lamps.

He has a house.

It contains many indications of Empire: small silk Union Jacks, a red-blotched map of the world, Pears' Soap, Epps's Cocoa, Lea & Perrin's Sauce, a chromo-lithograph of Edward VII and Queen Alexandra, Beecham's Pills, Mazzawattee Tea canisters and, stamped in purple inside wardrobes and drawers, the assurance *Manufactured by European Labour Only*. The house contains also many indications of a lower middle-class lavishness Australians regard as bare necessities. In the meat-safe are a sirloin, pounds of rump steak and cutlets. In the pantry are a case of apples, a pineapple, peaches, oranges and bananas.

The shelves are lined with bottles of jam, with sauces, pickles, chutneys and jars of Rose's Marmalade. On top of the crammed vegetable rack lies a crescent of pumpkin on the cut surface of which is some large back-to-front lettering sucked from the newspaper it was wrapped in. This may be, for all I know, the heading from the news of the Czar of Russia's assassination. It is curious that these mundane and humbly lavish still lifes of food should be so clearly remembered for, never having experienced what hunger is, I have no recollection of ever performing, at that time, the act of eating anything except mandarins, strawberries and asparagus. There is my wooden egg-cup, my own egg-spoon with teeth-dents in its silver bowl, and no memory of egg-eating. There is the Sunday tea-table: white damask glossily starched, and bearing, as the table-napkins stiff as cardboard do, a design of swans and bulrushes; the salad bowl, cake-stands, jam dishes, pickle jars, sugar-castor and celery vase all of cut glass; the tiered electro-plated cruet; the silver trumpets of sweet peas; the butter knives, cake knives, jam spoons and Sunday bread-knife with mother-of-pearl handles, and silver-gilt blades and bowls engraved with florid scrolls and curly acanthus leaves – all the glitter and gleam of the setting for an Australian Sunday tea. I recall seeing the emerald green jellies inside whose fluted trembling are suspended grapes and strawberries and banana slices; the pink-iced sponge-cakes flavoured with rose-water, the cream puffs, macaroons and lamingtons piled up; the ham coated in breadcrumbs and stuck with cloves at Father's end of the table and, at Mother's end, the highly peppered Sargasso of sliced cucumber, tomato, lettuce, onion and radishes sodden in Champion's Malt Vinegar which Mother imagines is a salad. Although no memory of sitting at the table and eating remains I must, of course, have eaten like a little boy.

He is a little boy.

He has a sheep-dog called Nigger.

Mother has brought Nigger from the country along with her linen sheets, crochet-rimmed pillow-shams, tea-cosies, crested silver forks and teapot and table-spoons, Rockingham dinner service and a collection of aprons graded in size and material to match every domestic duty: black Italian cloth for sordid tasks, white bibbed ones for cleaner tasks, small useless ones heavily embroidered or inset and edged with lace for more ceremonial occasions, symbolic garments of no use and on which no spot is permitted to fall. Nigger, the one living object of the trousseau, is older than the boy, so many years older that his teeth are abraded almost to the gums. Bulky as a wrestler, Nigger prefers a pretence of drowsing and dreaming prone rather than levering a burden of body to its bored legs. Seeming as old as Grandfather, Nigger is not unoccupied as Grandfather is. Wisdom, sympathy, forbearance, and a weary knowledge of which shade of kindness a mood demands, occupy Nigger. The boy kisses him as one kisses life; reluctantly but of polite necessity to kiss Grandfather is to kiss death.

Besides Nigger he has toys. He has a no-eyed Teddy Bear he kisses more than Nigger or anyone, a glass walking-stick, a wooden top, a skewbald rocking-horse with a real horse's tail, a paint-box, a slate with a walnut of sponge attached by a string, Cole's Funny Picture Book, a large india-rubber ball decorated with a shiny picture of a fair-haired boy like him playing with a large india-rubber ball decorated with. . . . The implications of the ball thus decorated tempt him to thoughts of never-ending diminution, to his first thoughts on the nature of infinity. In later life this absurd game engages his attention for a period until he reins back his mind to the fact that he is to deny any donation of other impermanent animals to the pattern his parents, impermanent animals, have donated him to.

He has Mother and Father.

Fortified by these possessions, these seemingly indestructible possessions, his belly full, his body neutralized by excellent health and proper degrees of warmth, he is freed for timeless and solitary behaviour.

He has, above and beyond all and everyone else, himself.

He presses the palms of his hands firmly on his eyeballs to make the phosphenes glide from the luminously veined dark he has brought into being. Glowing oval blots, rimmed with a blurred electric blue, swim out of the ornamented gloom, then, on the point of capture, slip sideways and upwards out of vision, to be replaced by others and others and others, all infinitesimally different – stemless flowers of his own manufacture.

It rains. He sits, neatly as a story-book boy, on the colonial sofa in the living-room. He watches the drops on the pane. For how long? For a little while? To this moment; he sits there watching to this very moment. He sees the drops writing their descents on the glass, wriggling in a pretence that they avoid linking with other drops, next swiftly darting to snatch other drops, to melt together and stream dying out of sight. 'Gentle Annie,' says his mother of the rain, in an informing tone. And then, again, abstractedly, 'Gent-le An-nie,' as though listening, not to the present rain but to a bygone rain and something else. Is Mother, he thinks, listening to her own English mother saying, 'Gentle Annie'? He thinks of the fair boy playing with the ball on the ball he plays with.

It is a sunny day. He has looked at the green fruit on the backyard tomato bushes or at a snail or at the view or under Nigger's tail. Is there nowhere else to look in the world? 'Go and look up the chimney,' says Mother, reminding him of a pleasure he always forgets to remind himself of. He lies on the rag rug, his head on the raddled bricks of the fireplace. In the blue at the chimney-top he finds a daytime star. He watches it, and watches too the black miniature cauliflowers of soot bloomed with indigo that grow in the chimney tunnel. Oh, to grow there! he thinks. Oh, he yearns, to fly there and nestle in the blue-black!

He looks out through the coloured glass panels of the living-room door, first at a ruby-tinged world, then at a yellow one, finally at a world blue as the blue of a castor-oil bottle. Oh, to walk there, to watch himself walk there, wandering off and away, the blue-haired boy holding the blue Teddy Bear, and disappearing among the boles of the blue plane-trees.

Hal Porter *The Watcher on the Cast-Iron Balcony*

Growing

Small and little and does not know
about anything in the outside world.
Thinking everything is taller than him which
he is smaller. He is small with a
heavy face in place of a big tummy
then he sees smaller things he is
taller now. He thinks he's a giant
which he is to all little insects.

Joseph Korner *aged 8*

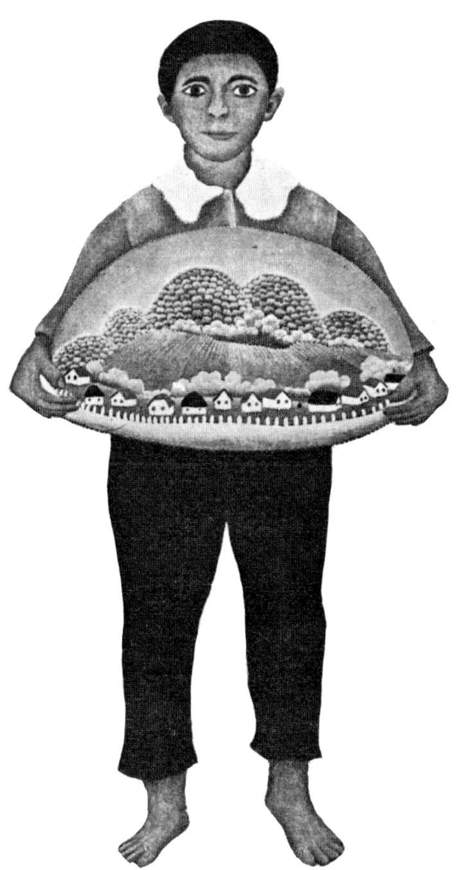

Why?

The twilight was white, and it lasted for a long while. Time in August could be divided into four parts: morning, afternoon, twilight and dark. At twilight the sky became a curious blue-green which soon faded to white. The air was soft grey, and the arbour and trees were slowly darkening. It was the hour when sparrows gathered and whirled above the rooftops of the town, and when in the darkened elms along the street there was the August sound of the cicadas. Noises at twilight had a blurred sound, and they lingered: the slam of a screen door down the street, voices of children, the whirr of a lawn mower from a yard somewhere. F. Jasmine brought in the evening newspaper, and dark was coming in the kitchen. The corners in the room at first were dark, then the drawing on the wall faded. The three of them watched the dark come on in silence.

'The army is now in Paris.'

'That's good.'

They were quiet awhile and then F. Jasmine said: 'I have a lot of things to do. I ought to start out now.'

But although she stood ready in the doorway, she did not go. On this last evening, the last time with the three of them together in the kitchen, she felt there was some final thing she ought to say or do before she went away. For many months she had been ready to leave this kitchen, never to return again; but now that the time had come, she stood there with her head and shoulder leaning against the door-jamb, somehow unready. It was the darkening hour when the remarks they made had a sad and beautiful sound, although there would be nothing sad or beautiful about the meanings of the words.

F. Jasmine said quietly: 'I intend to take two baths tonight. One long soaking bath and scrub with a brush. I'm going to try to scrape this brown crust off my elbows. Then let out the dirty water and take a second bath.'

'That's a good idea,' said Berenice. 'I will be glad to see you clean.'

'I will take another bath,' John Henry said. His voice was thin and sad; she could not see him in the darkening room, since he stood in the corner by the stove. At seven Berenice had bathed him and dressed him in his shorts again. She heard him shuffle carefully across the room, for after the bath he had put on Berenice's hat and was trying to walk in Berenice's high-heeled shoes. Again he asked a question which by itself meant nothing. 'Why?' he asked.

'Why what, Baby?' said Berenice.

He did not answer, and it was F. Jasmine who finally said: 'Why is it against the law to change your name?'

Berenice sat in a chair against the pale white light of the window. She held the newspaper before her, and her head was twisted down and to one side as she strained to see what was printed there. When F. Jasmine spoke, she folded the paper and put it away on the table.

'You can figure that out,' she said. 'Just because. Think of the confusion.'

'I don't see why,' F. Jasmine said.

'What is that on your neck?' said Berenice. 'I thought it was a head you carried on that neck. Just think. Suppose I would suddenly up and call myself Mrs Eleanor Roosevelt. And you would begin naming yourself Joe Louis. And John Henry would try to pass off as Henry Ford. Now what kind of confusion do you think that would cause?'

'Don't talk childish,' F. Jasmine said. 'That is not the kind of changing I mean. I mean from a name that doesn't suit you to a name you prefer. Like I changed from Frankie to F. Jasmine.'

'But still it would be a confusion,' Berenice insisted. 'Suppose we all suddenly change to entirely different names. Nobody would ever know who anybody was talking about. The whole world would go crazy.'

'I don't see –'

'Because things accumulate around your name,' said Berenice. 'You have a name and one thing after another happens to you, and you behave in various ways and do things, so that soon the name begins to have a meaning. Things have accumulated around the name. If it is bad and you have a bad reputation, then you just can't jump out of your name and escape like that. And if it is good and you have a good reputation, then you should be content and satisfied.'

'But what had accumulated around my old name?' F. Jasmine asked. Then, when Berenice did not reply at once, F. Jasmine answered her own question. 'Nothing! See? My name just didn't mean anything.'

'Well, that's not exactly so,' said Berenice. 'People think of Frankie Addams and it brings to the mind that Frankie is finished with the B section of the seventh grade. And Frankie found the golden egg at the Baptist Easter Hunt. And Frankie lives on Grove Street and –'

'But those things are nothing,' F. Jasmine said. 'See? They're not worth while. Nothing ever happened to me.'

'But it will,' said Berenice. 'Things will happen.'

'What?' F. Jasmine asked.

Berenice sighed and reached for the Chesterfield package inside her bosom. 'You pin me down like that and I can't tell you truthfully. If I could I would be a wizard. I wouldn't be sitting here in this kitchen right now, but making a fine living on Wall Street as a wizard. All I can say is that things will happen. Just what, I don't know.'

'By the way,' F. Jasmine said after a while. 'I thought I would go around to your house and see Big Mama. I don't believe in those fortunes, or anything like that, but I thought I might as well.'

'Suit yourself. However, I don't think it is necessary.'

'I suppose I ought to leave now,' F. Jasmine said.

But still she waited in the darkening door and did not go away. The sounds of the summer twilight crossed within the silence of the kitchen. Mr Schwarzenbaum had finished tuning the piano, and for the past quarter of an hour he had been playing little pieces. He played music memorized by note, and he was a nervous spry old man who reminded F. Jasmine of a silver spider. His music was spry and stiff also, and he played faint jerking waltzes and nervous lullabies. Farther down the block a solemn radio announced something they could not hear. In the O'Neils's back yard, next door, children were calling and swatting a ball. The sounds of evening cancelled out each other, and they were faded in the darkening twilight air. The kitchen itself was very quiet.

'Listen,' F. Jasmine said. 'What I've been trying to say is this. Doesn't it strike you as strange that I am I, and you are you? I am F. Jasmine Addams. And you are Berenice Sadie Brown. And we can look at each other, and touch each other, and stay together year in and year out in the same room. Yet always I am I, and you are you. And I can't ever be anything else but me, and you can't ever be anything else but you. Have you ever thought of that? And does it seem to you strange?'

Berenice had been rocking slightly in the chair. She was not sitting in a rocking chair, but she had been tilting back in the straight chair, then letting the front legs hit the floor with little taps, her dark stiff hand held to the table edge for balance. She stopped rocking herself when F. Jasmine spoke. And finally she said: 'I have thought of it occasionally.'

It was the hour when the shapes in the kitchen darkened and voices bloomed. They spoke softly and their voices bloomed like flowers – if sounds can be like flowers and voices bloom. F. Jasmine stood with her hands clasped behind her head, facing the darkening room. She had the feeling that unknown words were in her throat, and she was ready to speak them. Strange words were flowering in her throat and now was the time for her to name them.

'This,' she said. 'I see a green tree. And to me it is green. And you would call the tree green also. And we would agree on this. But is this colour you see as green the same colour I see as green? Or say we both call a colour black. But how do we know that what you see as black is the same colour I see as black?'

Berenice said after a moment: 'Those things we just cannot prove.'

F. Jasmine scraped her head against the door, and put her hand up to her throat. Her voice shattered and died. 'That's not what I meant to say, anyway.'

The smoke of Berenice's cigarette lay bitter and warm and stagnant in the room. John Henry shuffled in the high-heeled shoes from the stove to the table and back again. A rat rattled behind the wall.

'This is what I mean,' F. Jasmine said. 'You are walking down a street and you meet somebody. Anybody. And you look at each other. And you are you. And he is him. Yet when you look at each other, the eyes make a connection. Then you go off one way. And he goes off another way. You go off into different parts of town, and maybe you never see each other again. Not in your whole life. Do you see what I mean?'

'Not exactly,' said Berenice.

'I'm talking about this town,' F. Jasmine said in a higher voice. 'There are all these people here I don't even know by sight or name. And we pass alongside each other and don't have any connection. And they don't know me and I don't know them. And now I'm leaving town and there are all these people I will never know.'

'But who do you want to know?' asked Berenice.

F. Jasmine answered: 'Everybody. In the world. Everybody in the world.'

'Why, I wish you would listen to that,' said Berenice. 'How about people like Willis Rhodes? How about them Germans? Them Japanese?'

F. Jasmine knocked her head against the door-jamb and looked up at the dark ceiling. Her voice broke, and again she said: 'That's not what I mean. That's not what I'm talking about.'

'Well, what *is* you talking about?' asked Berenice.

F. Jasmine shook her head, almost as though she did not know. Her heart was dark and silent, and from her heart the unknown words flowered and bloomed and she waited to name them. From next door there was the evening sound of children's baseball and the long call: Batteruup! Batteruup! Then the hollow pock of a ball and the clatter of a thrown bat and running footsteps and wild voices. The window was a rectangle of pale clear light and a child ran across the yard and under the dark arbour after the ball. The child was quick as a shadow and F. Jasmine did not see his face – his white shirt-tails flapped loose behind him like queer wings. Beyond the window the twilight was lasting and pale and still.

Carson McCullers *The Member of the Wedding*

Reference Back

That was a pretty one, I heard you call
From the unsatisfactory hall
To the unsatisfactory room where I
Played record after record, idly,
Wasting my time at home, that you
Looked so much forward to.

Oliver's *Riverside Blues*, it was. And now
I shall, I suppose, always remember how
The flock of notes those antique negroes blew
Out of Chicago air into
A huge remembering pre-electric horn
The year after I was born
Three decades later made this sudden bridge
From your unsatisfactory age
To my unsatisfactory prime.

Truly, though our element is time,
We are not suited to the long perspectives
Open at each instant of our lives.
They link us to our losses: worse,
They show us what we have as it once was,
Blindingly undiminished, just as though
By acting differently we could have kept it so.

Philip Larkin

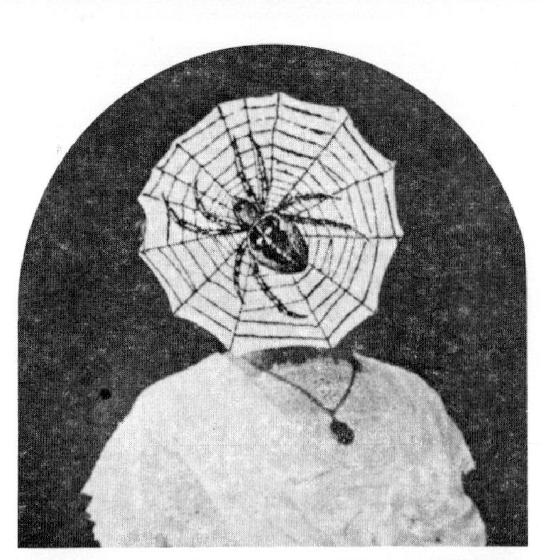

Persons, Relations and Families

We are concerned with persons, the relations between persons, and the characteristics of the family as a system composed of a multiplicity of persons. Our theoretical position with particular respect to our method, is as follows.

Each person not only is an object in the world of others but is a position in space and time from which he experiences, constitutes and acts in *his* world. He is his own centre with his own point of view, and it is precisely each person's *perspective* on the situation that he shares with others that we wish to discover.

However, each person does not occupy a single definable position in relation to other members of his or her own family. . . .

Let us suppose that Jill has a father and mother and brother who all live together. If one wishes to form a complete picture of her as a family person, let alone as a person outside the family, it will be necessary to see how she experiences and acts in all the following contexts:

Jill alone
Jill with mother
Jill with father
Jill with brother
Jill with mother and father
Jill with mother and brother
Jill with father and brother
Jill with mother, father and brother.

One sees that it is a fairly crude differentiation of the various positions that Jill has to adopt to characterize them as daughter or sister.

Samples of behaviour require to be taken of each person in the family in turn in the same way. People have identities. But they may also change quite remarkably as they become different others-to-others. It is arbitrary to regard any one of these transformations or alterations as basic, and the others as variations.

Not only may the one person behave differently in his different alterations, but he may experience himself in different ways. He is liable to remember different things, express different attitudes, even quite discordant ones, imagine and fantasize in different ways, and so on.

R. D. Laing and **A. Esterson** *Sanity, Madness and the Family*

Roles

Every role in society has attached to it a certain identity. As we have seen, some of these identities are trivial and temporary ones, as in some occupations that demand little modification in the being of their practitioners. It is not difficult to change from garbage collector to night watchman. It is considerably more difficult to change from clergyman to officer. It is very, very difficult to change from Negro to white. And it is almost impossible to change from man to woman.

These differences in the case of role changing ought not to blind us to the fact that even identities that we consider to be our essential selves have been socially assigned. Just as there are racial roles to be acquired and identified with, so there are sexual roles. To say 'I am a man' is just as much a proclamation of role as to say 'I am a colonel in the US Army'. We are well aware of the fact that one is born a male, while not even the most humourless martinet imagines himself to have been born with a golden eagle sitting on his umbilical cord. But to be biologically male is a far cry from the specific, socially defined (and, of course, socially relative) role that goes with the statement 'I am a man'. A male child does not have to learn to have an erection. But he must learn to be aggressive, to have ambitions, to compete with others, and to be suspicious of too much gentleness in himself. The male role in our society, however, requires all these things that one must learn, as does a male identity. To have an erection is not enough – if it were, regiments of psychotherapists would be out of work.

This significance of role theory could be summarized by saying that, in a sociological perspective, identity is socially bestowed, socially sustained and socially transformed. The example of the man in process of becoming an officer may suffice to illustrate the way in which identities are bestowed in adult life. However, even roles that are much more fundamentally part of what psychologists would call our personality than those associated with a particular adult activity are bestowed in very similar manner through a social process. This has been demonstrated over and over again in studies of so-called socialization – the process by which a child learns to be a participant member of society.

Probably the most penetrating theoretical account of this process is the one given by Mead, in which the genesis of the self is interpreted as being one and the same event as the discovery of society. The child finds out who he is as he learns what society is. He learns to play roles properly belonging to him by learning, as Mead put it, 'to take the role of the other' – which, incidentally, is the crucial socio-psychological function of play, in which children masquerade with a variety of social roles and in doing so discover the significance of those being assigned to them. All this learning occurs, and can only occur, in interaction with other human beings, be it the parents or whoever else raises the child. The child first takes on roles *vis-à-vis* what Mead calls his 'significant others', that is, those persons who deal with him intimately and whose attitudes are decisive for the formation of his conception of himself. Later, the child learns that the roles he plays are not only relevant to this intimate circle, but relate to the expectations directed toward him by society at large. This higher level of abstraction in the social response Mead calls the discovery of the 'generalized other'. That is, not only the child's mother expects him to be good, clean and truthful, society in general does so as well. Only when this general conception of society emerges is the child capable of forming a clear conception of himself. 'Self' and 'society', in the child's experience, are the two sides of the same coin.

In other words, identity is not something 'given', but is bestowed in acts of social recognition. We become that as which we are addressed. The same idea is expressed in Cooley's well-known description of the self as a reflection in a looking glass. This does not mean, of course, that there are not certain characteristics an individual is born with, that are carried by his genetic heritage regardless of the social environment in which the latter will have to unfold itself. Our knowledge of man's biology does not as yet allow us a very clear picture of the extent to which this may be true. We do know, however, that the room for social formation within those genetic limits is very large indeed. Even with the biological questions left largely unsettled, we can say that to be human is to be recognized as human, just as to be a certain kind of man is to be recognized as such. The child deprived of human affection and attention becomes dehumanized. The child who is given respect comes to respect himself. A little boy considered to be a *schlemiel* becomes one, just as a grown-up treated as an awe-inspiring young god of war begins to think of himself and act as is appropriate to such a figure – and, indeed, merges his identity with the one he is presented with in these expectations.

scoundrel

Identities are socially bestowed. They must also be socially sustained, and fairly steadily so. One cannot be human all by oneself and, apparently, one cannot hold on to any particular identity all by oneself. The self-image of the officer as an officer can be maintained only in a social context in which others are willing to recognize him in this identity. If this recognition is suddenly withdrawn, it usually does not take very long before the self-image collapses.

Cases of radical withdrawal of recognition by society can tell us much about the social character of identity. For example, a man turned overnight from a free citizen into a convict finds himself subjected at once to a massive assault on his previous conception of himself. He may try desperately to hold on to the latter, but in the absence of others in his immediate environment confirming his old identity he will find it almost impossible to maintain it within his own consciousness. With frightening speed he will discover that he is acting as a convict is supposed to, and feeling all the things that a convict is expected to feel. It would be a misleading perspective on this process to look upon it simply as one of the disintegration of personality. A more accurate way of seeing the phenomenon is as a reintegration of personality, no different in its socio-psychological dynamics from the process in which the old identity was integrated. It used to be that our man was treated by all the important people around him as responsible, dignified, considerate and aesthetically fastidious. Consequently he was able to be all these things. Now the walls of the prison separate him from those whose recognition sustained him in the exhibition of these traits. Instead he is now surrounded by people who treat him as irresponsible, swinish in behaviour, only out for his own interests and careless of his appearance unless forced to take care by constant supervision. The new expectations are typified in the convict role that responds to them just as the old ones were integrated into a different pattern of conduct. In both cases, identity comes with conduct and conduct occurs in response to a specific social situation.

Extreme cases in which an individual is radically stripped of his old identity simply illustrate more sharply processes that occur in ordinary life. We live our everyday lives within a complex web of recognitions and non-recognitions. We work better when we are given encouragement by our superiors. We find it hard to be anything but clumsy in a gathering where we know people have an image of us as awkward. We become wits when people expect us to be funny, and interesting characters when we know that such a reputation has preceded us; intelligence, humour, manual skills, religious devotion and even sexual potency respond with equal alacrity to the expectations of others. This makes understandable the previously mentioned process by which individuals choose their associates in such a way that the latter sustain their self-interpretations. To put this succinctly, every act of social affiliation entails a choice of identity. Conversely every identity requires specific social affiliations for its survival. Birds of the same feather flock together not as a luxury but out of necessity. The intellectual becomes a slob after he is kidnapped by the army. The theological student progressively loses his sense of humour as he approaches ordination. The worker who breaks all norms finds that he breaks even more after he has been given a medal by management. The young man with anxieties about his virility becomes hell-on-wheels in bed when he finds a girl who sees him as an avatar of Don Giovanni.

Peter L. Berger *Invitation to Sociology*

Personal Names Tabooed

Unable to discriminate clearly between words and things, the savage commonly fancies that the link between a name and the person or thing denominated by it is not a mere arbitrary and ideal association, but a real and substantial bond which unites the two in such a way that magic may be wrought on a man just as easily through his name as through his hair, his nails, or any other material part of his person. In fact, primitive man regards his name as a vital portion of himself and takes care of it accordingly. Thus, for example, the North American Indian

regards his name, not as a mere label, but as a distinct part of his personality, just as much as are his eyes or his teeth, and believes that injury will result as surely from the malicious handling of his name as from a wound inflicted on any part of his physical organism. This belief was found among the various tribes from the Atlantic to the Pacific and has occasioned a number of curious regulations in regard to the concealment and change of names.

Some Esquimaux take new names when they are old, hoping thereby to get a new lease of life. The Tolampoos of Celebes believe that if you write a man's name down you can carry off his soul along with it. Many savages at the present day regard their names as vital parts of themselves, and therefore take great pains to conceal their real names, lest those should give to evil-disposed persons a handle by which to injure their owners.

Thus, to begin with the savages who rank at the bottom of the social scale, we are told that the secrecy with which among the Australian aborigines personal names are often kept from general knowledge 'arises in great measure from the belief that an enemy, who knows your name, has in it something which he can use magically to your detriment'. . . . Amongst the tribes of Central Australia every man, woman and child has, besides a personal name which is in common use, a secret or sacred name which is bestowed by the older men upon him or her soon after birth, and which is known to none but the fully initiated members of the group. This secret name is never mentioned except upon the most solemn occasions; to utter it in the hearing of women or of men of another group would be a most serious breach of tribal custom, as serious as the most flagrant case of sacrilege among ourselves. When mentioned at all, the name is spoken only in a whisper, and not until the most elaborate precautions have been taken that it shall be heard by no one but members of the group. 'The native thinks that a stranger knowing his secret name would have special power to work him ill by means of magic.'. . .

The Indians of Chiloe keep their names secret and do not like to have them uttered aloud; for they say that there are fairies or imps on the mainland or neighbouring islands who, if they knew folks' names, would do them an injury: but so long as they do not know the names, these mischievous sprites are powerless. The Araucanians will hardly ever tell a stranger their names because they fear that he would thereby

acquire some supernatural power over themselves. Asked his name by a stranger, who is ignorant of their superstitions, an Araucanian will answer, 'I have none.' When an Ojebway is asked his name, he will look at some bystander and ask him to answer.

This reluctance arises from an impression they receive when young, that if they repeat their own names it will prevent their growth, and they will be small in stature. On account of this unwillingness to tell their names, many strangers have fancied that they either have no names or have forgotten them.

In this last case no scruple seems to be felt about communicating a man's name to strangers, and no ill effects to be dreaded as a consequence of divulging it; harm is only done when a name is spoken by its owner. Why is this? and why in particular should a man be thought to stunt his growth by uttering his own name? We may conjecture that to savages who act and think thus a person's name only seems to be a part of himself when it is uttered with his own breath; uttered by the breath of others it has no vital connection with him, and no harm can come to him through it. Whereas, so these primitive philosophers may have argued, when a man lets his own name pass his lips, he is parting with a living piece of himself, and if he persists in so reckless a course he must certainly end by dissipating his energy and shattering his constitution.

Sir James Frazer *The Golden Bough*

The Overloaded Man

His programme usually followed the same course. First, from the centre drawer of his desk he took a small alarm clock, fitted with a battery and wrist strap. Sitting down on the veranda, he fastened the strap to his wrist, wound and set the clock and placed it on the table next to him, binding his arm to the chair so that there was no danger of dragging the clock on to the floor.

Ready now, he lay back and surveyed the scene in front of him.

Menninger Village, or the 'Bin' as it was known locally, had been built about ten years earlier as a self-contained housing unit for the graduate staff of the Clinic and their families. In all there were some sixty houses in the development, each designed to fit into a particular architectonic niche, preserving its own identity from within and at the same time merging into the organic unity of the whole development. The object of the architects, faced with the task of compressing a great number of small houses into a four-acre site, had been, firstly to avoid producing a collection of identical hutches, as in most housing estates, and secondly, to provide a showpiece for a major psychiatric foundation which would serve as a model for the corporate living units of the future.

However, as everyone there had found out, living in the Bin was hell on earth. The architects had employed the so-called psycho-modular system – a basic L-design – and this meant that everything under- or overlapped everything else, the whole development was a sprawl of interlocking frosted glass, white rectangles and curves, at first glance exciting and abstract (*Life* magazine had done several glossy photographic treatments of the new 'living trends' suggested by the Village) but to the people within formless and visually exhausting. Most of the Clinic's senior staff had soon taken off, and the Village was now let out to anyone who could be persuaded to live there.

Faulkner gazed out across the veranda, separating from the clutter of white geometric shapes thc cight other houses he could see without moving his head. On his left, immediately adjacent, were the Penzils, with the McPhersons on the right; the other six houses were directly ahead, on the far side of a muddle of interlocking garden areas, abstract rat-runs divided by waist-high white panelling, glass angle-pieces and slatted screens.

In the Penzils's garden was a collection of huge alphabet blocks, each three feet high, which their two children played with. Often they left messages out on the grass for Faulkner to read, sometimes obscene, at others merely gnomic and obscure. This morning's came into the latter category. The blocks spelled out:

STOP AND GO

Speculating on the total significance of this statement, Faulkner let his mind relax, his eyes staring blankly at the houses. Gradually their already obscured outlines began to merge and fade, the long balconies and ramps partly hidden by the intervening trees became disembodied forms, like gigantic geometric units.

Breathing slowly, Faulkner steadily closed his mind, then without any effort erased his awareness of the identity of the houses opposite.

He was now looking at a cubist landscape, a collection of random white forms below a blue backdrop, across which several powdery green blurs moved slowly backwards and forwards. Idly, he wondered what these geometric forms really represented – he knew that only a few seconds earlier they had constituted an immediately familiar part of his everyday existence – but however he rearranged them spatially in his mind, or sought their associations, they still remained a random assembly of geometric forms.

He had discovered this talent only about three weeks ago. Balefully eyeing the silent television set in the lounge one Sunday morning he had suddenly realized that he had so completely accepted and assimilated the physical form of the plastic cabinet that he could no longer remember its function. It had required a considerable mental effort to recover himself and re-identify it. Out of interest he had tried out the new talent on other objects, found that it was particularly successful with over-associated ones such as washing machines, cars and other consumer goods. Stripped of their accretions of sales slogans and status imperatives, their real claim to reality was so tenuous that it needed little mental effort to obliterate them altogether.

The effect was similar to that of mescaline and other hallucinogens, under whose influence the dents in a cushion became as vivid as the craters of the moon, the folds in a curtain the ripples in the waves of eternity.

During the following weeks Faulkner had experimented carefully, training his ability to operate the cut-out switches. The process was slow, but gradually he found himself able to eliminate larger and larger groups of objects, the mass-produced furniture in the lounge, the over-enamelled gadgets in the kitchen, his car in the garage – de-identified, it sat in the half-light like an enormous vegetable marrow, flaccid and gleaming; trying to identify it had driven him almost out of his mind. 'What on earth could it *possibly* be?' he had asked himself helplessly, splitting his sides with laughter – and as the facility developed he had dimly perceived that here was an escape route from the intolerable world in which he found himself at the village.

He had described the facility to Ross Hendricks, who lived a few houses away, also a lecturer at the Business School and Faulkner's only close friend.

'I may actually be stepping out of time,' Faulkner speculated. 'Without a time-sense consciousness is difficult to visualize. That is, eliminating the vector of time from the de-identified object frees it from all its everyday cognitive associations. Alternatively, I may have stumbled on a means of repressing the photo-associative centres that normally identify visual objects, in the same way that you can so listen to someone speaking your own language that none of the sounds has any meaning. Everyone's tried this at some time.'

Hendricks had nodded. 'But don't make a career out of it, though.' He eyed Faulkner carefully. 'You can't simply turn a blind eye to the world. The subject-object relationship is not as polar as Descartes' *Cogito ergo sum* suggests. By any degree to which you devalue the external world so you devalue yourself. It seems to me that your real problem is to reverse the process.'

But Hendricks, however sympathetic, was beyond helping Faulkner. Besides, it was pleasant to see the world afresh again, to wallow in an endless panorama of brilliantly coloured images. What did it matter if there was form but no content –?

J. G. Ballard

Glass and the Ego

If the outward world was changed by glass, the inner world was likewise modified. Glass has a profound effect upon the development of the personality: indeed, it helped to alter the very concept of the self.

In a small way, glass had been used for mirrors by the Romans; but the background was a dark one, and the image was no more plain than it had been on the polished metal surface. By the sixteenth century, even before the invention of plate glass that followed a hundred years later, the mechanical surface of the glass had been improved to such an extent that, by coating it with a silver amalgam, an excellent mirror could be created. Technically this was, according to Schulz, perhaps the highest point in Venetian glass-making. Large mirrors, accordingly, became relatively cheap and the hand-mirror became a common possession.

For perhaps the first time, except for reflections in the water and in the dull surfaces of metal mirrors, it was possible to find an image that corresponded accurately to what others saw. Not merely in the privacy of the boudoir: in another's home, in a public gathering, the image of the ego in new and unexpected attitudes accompanied one. The most powerful prince of the seventeenth century created a vast hall of mirrors, and the mirror spread from one room to another in the bourgeois household. Self-consciousness, introspection, mirror-conversation developed with the new object itself: this preoccupation with one's image comes at the threshold of the mature personality when young Narcissus gazes long and deep into the face of the pool – and the sense of the separate personality, a perception of the objective attributes of one's identity, grows out of this communion.

The use of the mirror signalled the beginning of introspective biography in the modern style: that is, not as a means of edification but as a picture of the self, its depths, its

mysteries, its inner dimensions. The self in the mirror corresponds to the physical world that was brought to light by natural science in the same epoch: it was the self *in abstracto,* only part of the real self, the part that one can divorce from the background of nature and the influential presence of other men. But there is a value in this mirror personality that more naïve cultures did not possess. If the image one sees in the mirror is abstract, it is not ideal or mythical: the more accurate the physical instrument, the more sufficient the light on it, the more relentlessly does it show the effects of age, disease, disappointment, frustration, slyness, covetousness, weakness – these come out quite as clearly as health and joy and confidence. Indeed, when one is completely whole and at one with the world one does not need the mirror: it is in the period of psychic disintegration that the individual personality turns to the lonely image to see what in fact is there and what he can hold on to; and it was in the period of cultural disintegration that men began to hold the mirror up to outer nature.

Who is the greatest of the introspective biographers? Where does one find him? It is none other than Rembrandt, and it is no accident that he was a Hollander. Rembrandt had a robust interest in the doctors and burghers about him: as a young man he was still enough of a guildsman and still had enough of the corporate personality to make a pass at painting those collective portraits which the members of the Nightwatch or the College of Physicians might commission – although already he was playing tricks with their conventions. But he came to the core of his art in the series of self-portraits he painted: for it was partly from the face he found in the mirror, from the knowledge of himself he developed and expressed in this communion, that he achieved the insight he applied to other men.

Lewis Mumford *Technics and Civilization*

Mirror

I am silver and exact. I have no preconceptions.
Whatever I see I swallow immediately
Just as it is, unmisted by love or dislike.
I am not cruel, only truthful –
The eye of a little god, four-cornered.
Most of the time I meditate on the opposite wall.
It is pink, with speckles. I have looked at it so long
I think it is a part of my heart. But it flickers.
Faces and darkness separate us over and over.

Now I am a lake. A woman bends over me,
Searching my reaches for what she really is.
Then she turns to those liars, the candles or the moon.
I see her back, and reflect it faithfully.
She rewards me with tears and an agitation of hands.
I am important to her. She comes and goes.
Each morning it is her face that replaces the darkness.
In me she has drowned a young girl, and in me an old woman
Rises toward her day after day, like a terrible fish.

Sylvia Plath

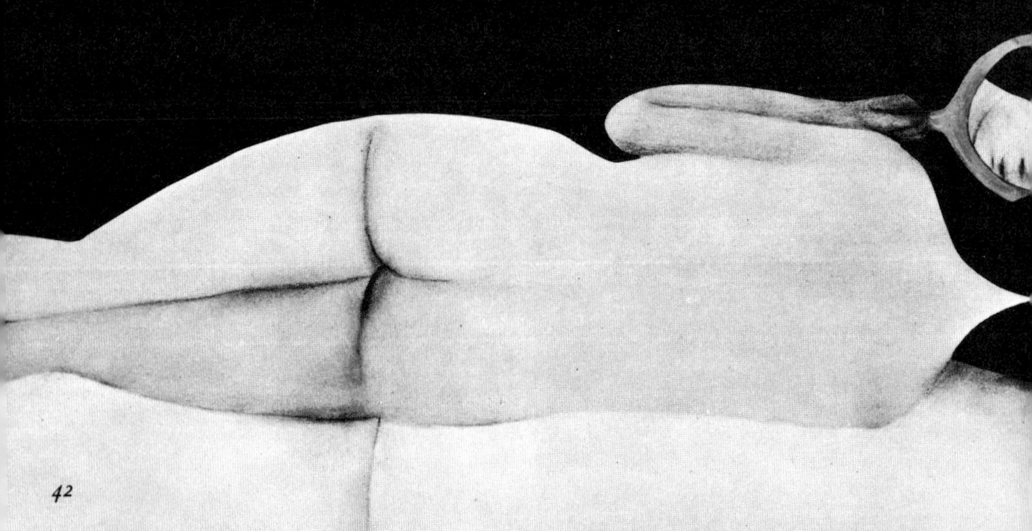

Mirror

I am silver and exact. I have no preconceptions.
Whatever I see I swallow immediately
Just as it is, unmisted by love or dislike.
I am not cruel, only truthful –
The eye of a little god, four-cornered.
Most of the time I meditate on the opposite wall.
It is pink, with speckles. I have looked at it so long
I think it is a part of my heart. But it flickers.
Faces and darkness separate us over and over.

Now I am a lake. A woman bends over me,
Searching my reaches for what she really is.
Then she turns to those liars, the candles or the moon.
I see her back, and reflect it faithfully.
She rewards me with tears and an agitation of hands.
I am important to her. She comes and goes.
Each morning it is her face that replaces the darkness.
In me she has drowned a young girl, and in me an old woman
Rises toward her day after day, like a terrible fish.

Sylvia Plath

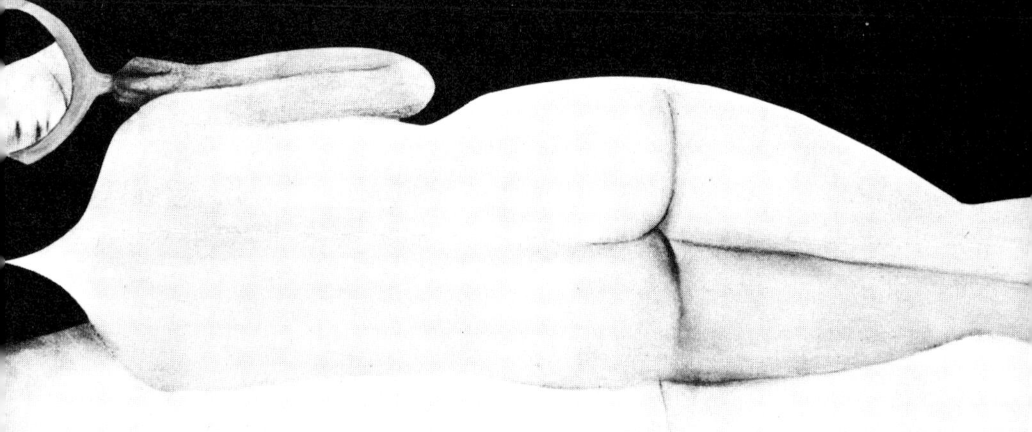

The Birth of Furriskey

Shorthand note of a cross-examination of Mr Trellis at a later date on the occasion of his being on trial for his life, the birth of Furriskey being the subject of the examination referred to:

In what manner was he born?

He awoke as if from sleep.

His sensations?

Bewilderment, perplexity.

Are not these terms synonymous and one as a consequence redundant?

Yes: but the terms of the inquiry postulated unsingular information.

(At this reply ten of the judges made angry noises on the counter with the butts of their stout-glasses. Judge Shanahan put his head out through a door and issued a severe warning to the witness, advising him to conduct himself and drawing his attention to the serious penalties which would be attendant on further impudence.)

His sensations? Is it not possible to be more precise?

It is. He was consumed by doubts as to his own identity, as to the nature of his body and the cast of his countenance.

In what manner did he resolve these doubts?

By the sensory perception of his ten fingers.

By feeling?

Yes.

Did you write the following: Sir Francis Thumb Drake, comma, with three inquiring midshipmen and a cabin boy, comma, he dispatched in a wrinkled Mayflower across the seas of his Braille face?

I did.

I put it to you that the passage was written by Mr Tracy and that you stole it.

No.

I put it to you that you are lying.

No.

Describe this man's conduct after he had examined his face.

He arose from his bed and examined his stomach, lower chest and legs.

What parts did he not examine?

His back, neck and head.

Can you suggest a reason for so imperfect a survey?

Yes. His vision was necessarily limited by the movement of his neck.

(At this point Judge Shanahan entered the court adjusting his dress and said: That point was exceedingly well taken. Proceed.)

Having examined his stomach, legs and lower chest, what did he do next?

He dressed.

He dressed? A suit of the latest pattern, made to measure?

No. A suit of navy-blue of the pre-war style.

With a vent behind?

Yes.

The cast-aways of your own wardrobe?

Yes.

I put it to you that your intention was purely to humiliate him.

No. By no means.

And after he was dressed in his ludicrous clothes . . . ?

He spent some time searching in his room for a looking-glass or for a surface that would enable him to ascertain the character of his countenance.

You had already hidden the glass?

No. I had forgotten to provide one.

By reason of his doubt as to his personal appearance, he suffered considerable mental anguish?

It is possible.

You could have appeared to him – by magic if necessary – and explained his identity and duties to him. Why did you not perform so obvious an errand of mercy?

I do not know.

Answer the question, please.

(At this point Judge Sweeny made an angry noise with a crack of his stout-glass on the counter and retired in a hurried petulant manner from the court.)

I suppose I fell asleep.

I see. You fell asleep.

Conclusion of the foregoing.

Flann O'Brien *At Swim-Two-Birds*

The Gigantic Mirror

He turned me about so that I faced the gigantic mirror on the wall. There I saw myself.

I saw myself for a brief instant as my usual self, except that I looked unusually good-humoured, bright and laughing. But I had scarcely had time to recognize myself before the reflection fell to pieces. A second, a third, a tenth, a twentieth figure sprang from it till the whole gigantic mirror was full of nothing but Harrys or bits of him, each of which I saw only for the instant of recognition. Some of these multitudinous Harrys were as old as I, some older, some very old. Others were young. There were youths, boys, schoolboys, scamps, children. Fifty year olds and twenty year olds played leap frog. Thirty year olds, solemn and merry, worthy and comic, well dressed and unpresentable, and even quite naked, long-haired and hairless, all were I and all were seen for a flash, recognized and gone. They sprang from each other in all directions, left and right and into the recesses of the mirror and clean out of it.

Hermann Hesse *Steppenwolf*

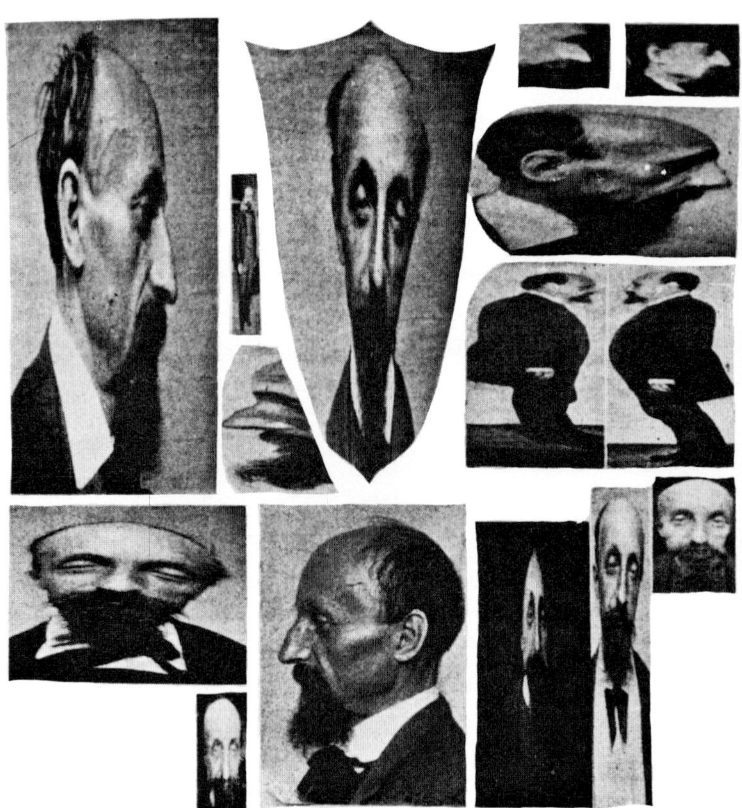

The Beast

Something that was not there before
has come through the mirror
into my room.

It is not such a simple creature
as at first I thought –
from somewhere it has brought a mischief

that troubles both silence and objects
and now left alone here
I weave intricate reasons for its arrival.

They disintegrate. Today in January, with
the light frozen on my window, I hear outside
a million panicking birds, and know even out there

comfort is done with; it has shattered
even the stars, this creature
at last come home to me.

Brian Patten

Among School Children

I

I walk through the long schoolroom questioning;
A kind old nun in a white hood replies;
The children learn to cipher and to sing,
To study reading-books and histories,
To cut and sew, be neat in everything
In the best modern way – the children's eyes
In momentary wonder stare upon
A sixty-year-old smiling public man.

II

I dream of a Ledaean body, bent
Above a sinking fire, a tale that she
Told of a harsh reproof, or trivial event
That changed some childish day to tragedy –
Told, and it seemed that our two natures blent
Into a sphere from youthful sympathy,
Or else, to alter Plato's parable,
Into the yolk and white of the one shell.

III

And thinking of that fit of grief or rage
I look upon one child or t'other there
And wonder if she stood so at that age –
For even daughters of the swan can share
Something of every paddler's heritage –
And had that colour upon cheek or hair,
And thereupon my heart is driven wild:
She stands before me as a living child.

IV

Her present image floats into the mind –
Did Quattrocento finger fashion it
Hollow of cheek as though it drank the wind
And took a mess of shadow for its meat?
And I though never of Ledaean kind
Had pretty plumage once – enough of that,
Better to smile on all that smile, and show
There is a comfortable kind of old scarecrow.

V

What youthful mother, a shape upon her lap
Honey of generation had betrayed,
And that must sleep, shriek, struggle to escape
As recollection or the drug decide,
Would think her son, did she but see that shape
With sixty or more winters on its head
A compensation for the pang of his birth,
Or the uncertainty of his setting forth?

VI

Plato thought nature but a spume that plays
Upon a ghostly paradigm of things;
Soldier Aristotle played the taws
Upon the bottom of a king of kings;
World-famous golden-thighed Pythagoras
Fingered upon a fiddle-stick or strings
What a star sang and careless Muses heard:
Old clothes upon old sticks to scare a bird.

VII

Both nuns and mothers worship images,
But those the candles light are not as those
That animate a mother's reveries,
But keep a marble or a bronze repose.
And yet they too break hearts – O Presences
That passion, piety or affection knows,
And that all heavenly glory symbolize –
O self-born mockers of man's enterprise;

VIII

Labour is blossoming or dancing where
The body is not bruised to pleasure soul,
Nor beauty born out of its own despair,
Nor blear-eyed wisdom out of midnight oil.
O chestnut-tree, great-rooted blossomer,
Are you the leaf, the blossom or the bole?
O body swayed to music, O brightening glance,
How can we know the dancer from the dance?

W. B. Yeats

Talking to a Stranger

FATHER You're happy, are you?

TERRY Yes. Why?

FATHER You should be happy.

[Terry walks across to the fireplace and stubs out the cigarette she brought in with her]

FATHER When are we going to see you again?

TERRY I don't know. Some time.

FATHER Soon. Your mother misses you.

TERRY Don't do too much. Don't let Alan break your back.

FATHER I won't.

TERRY He's on some sort of health kick.

FATHER What?

TERRY He's decided you need a lot of fresh air and exercise.

FATHER D'you remember that picnic?

TERRY Picnic? What picnic, Dad?

FATHER On a hill. The side of a hill – and you went running. You fell over!

TERRY Did that happen?

FATHER I thought you were going to roll – clear down the hill.

TERRY I thought I made it up.

FATHER It was such a hot day. Your mother had the devil of a job, making you keep your clothes on.

TERRY Funny.

FATHER D'you remember climbing? There was just the one path – and that wasn't much of a path.

TERRY I remember.

FATHER I had to carry you. Alan went on, up the path and stood . . .

[Silence]

He stood at the very top of the hill – and shouted down at us.

TERRY Yes.

FATHER 'Come on,' he shouted. 'Buck up.'

TERRY 'Slow-coaches.'

FATHER Your poor mother. She only just made it.

TERRY It was a good thing she did. She was carrying the food.

FATHER That was a day.

TERRY I thought I made it up.

FATHER That was a good day. Aren't you going to stay for supper?

TERRY No.

FATHER When are we going to see you again?

TERRY Oh – you know. Soon.

FATHER Yes. Make it soon.

TERRY I'll try to.

FATHER You were laughing and crying.

[The sound of a small child crying]

Dirt all over your face – your clothes. You cut your knee.

Cut to film. Looking down over the Father's shoulder, into the face of the child he is carrying. The child's face is dirty and slightly scratched. She is crying.

TERRY'S VOICE It was a good day.

FATHER'S VOICE Yes.

CHILD'S VOICE *[sobbing]* I hurt myself.

[Father scrambles up the slope, carefully.]

FATHER'S VOICE I told you, didn't I, poppet?

CHILD'S VOICE I didn't want to hurt myself.

[Long shot, looking down the slope, towards Father and the child in his arms.]

FATHER'S VOICE Scrambling about – and falling over. Running away! Didn't Daddy say? 'You'll hurt yourself.'

TERRY'S VOICE I didn't know it would hurt.

Cut to Terry's bedroom.

[Looking across the bed past Terry, at Father's silhouette]

TERRY He didn't tell me it would hurt. Nobody told me.

FATHER *[quietly]* What happened?

TERRY We went for a drive in his car.

FATHER Yes?

TERRY We went a long way – and it got late. I said, 'You must take me home' – and he laughed.

FATHER Where did you go?

TERRY I don't know. We went so fast. It – oh, it must've been a long way – and then, he stopped.

FATHER Yes?

TERRY He kissed me. He put his arms round me and held me – tight. He – then, he bit me – bit my ear and said things – whispered – things . . .

[Silence]

I said – 'Take me home' – and he laughed again.

FATHER What did he do?

TERRY He – pulled at me – pulled – at my dress – and tore it. I tried to get away from him – and all the time – Daddy – he was laughing all the time.

FATHER *[harshly]* What did he do?

TERRY *[childishly]* Hurt me.

FATHER *[harshly]* You – Terry – you let him . . .

TERRY *[fiercely]* Let him! No. I couldn't stop him.

[Silence]

FATHER How far did he – how . . .

TERRY He talked to me – all the time – whispering in my ear – gently – as if he was – telling me a story. Like you, Dad.

FATHER No.

TERRY Some secret – story.

FATHER Not – oh, no – not like . . . *[Father breaks away from Terry. He pulls away from her, completely]* No!

TERRY I could feel his hands – on me – over me. All – over me.

FATHER How could you let him – touch – Terry!

TERRY It didn't seem – I don't know – listening to him – listening to what he was saying – soft things, tender things – love . . .

[Terry reaches out towards her Father and he jerks farther away from her, along the bed]

Daddy?

FATHER You let him make – you – how could you . . .

TERRY I didn't want him to stop. I didn't – oh, it was so – real – and everything else – nothing!

FATHER I hate you.

TERRY Floating – drifting – and his hands – all I could feel . . .

FATHER Stop it.

TERRY All – I could hear . . .

FATHER Stop talking – stop . . .

TERRY Then – and then – he hurt me. I cried out.

[The sound of a woman's sudden cry of physical pain]

Cut to a hotel bedroom. Night.

[Looking across the large hotel room, towards the bed. The room is in darkness, except for the pattern of light striking across the floor, through the partially drawn curtains]

FATHER'S VOICE Sorry. I'm sorry. I didn't know. Sarah.

[Cut to a close-up of a young woman's face drenched in tears]

I didn't mean to hurt you. I wouldn't. Sarah, please – forgive me.

[The woman turns her face into the pillow, away from the sound of the voice]

For all the world, I wouldn't hurt . . .

[Cut to the long shot, looking across the room]

Sarah.

Cut to Terry's bedroom. Night.

FATHER'S VOICE Don't turn away.

TERRY He thought – he told me – afterwards . . .

FATHER I'll fetch your mother. *[Father stands up and turns away from the bed and Terry]*

TERRY No! Oh, no. Don't tell her.

FATHER You must talk – er . . .

TERRY It'll be all right. Look, he said . . . *[Terry scrambles on her knees in the bed]* Don't tell Mum.

FATHER *[mumbling]* Must – tell her.

TERRY I had to tell someone. I wanted to tell you.

FATHER Your mother – don't be silly – must . . .

TERRY I can't tell her.

[Father walks quickly towards the bedroom door]

FATHER Yes.

TERRY I won't.

FATHER We have to – tell your mother. She'll know – what to do.

[Father stumbles out of the room and on to the landing. He sways two or three steps and then lurches sideways against the wall. He presses his face flat to the wall and brings his hands up to his mouth. He retches and his body shudders. He crouches slightly, against the wall]

FATHER'S VOICE You've told your mother?

Cut to the back room.

TERRY Er – what?

FATHER You're not staying to supper.

TERRY Oh yes.

FATHER You know what she is. We've got your address, have we?

TERRY I'll give it to Mother.

FATHER Make sure you do.

[Silence]

TERRY 'Bye. *[Terry leans over and kisses her Father on the cheek]*

FATHER Take care of yourself.

John Hopkins

Night

[A woman and man in their forties. They sit with coffee.]

MAN I'm talking about that time by the river.

WOMAN What time?

MAN The first time. On the bridge. Starting on the bridge.

[Pause]

WOMAN I can't remember.

MAN On the bridge. We stopped and looked down at the river. It was night. There were lamps lit on the towpath. We were alone. We looked up the river. I put my hand on the small of your waist. Don't you remember? I put my hand under your coat.

[Pause]

WOMAN Was it winter?

MAN Of course it was winter. It was when we met. It was our first walk. You must remember that.

WOMAN I remember walking. I remember walking with you.

MAN The first time? Our first walk?

WOMAN Yes, of course I remember that.

[Pause]

WOMAN We walked down a road into a field, through some railings. We walked to a corner of the field and then we stood by the railings.

MAN It was on the bridge that we stopped.

[Pause]

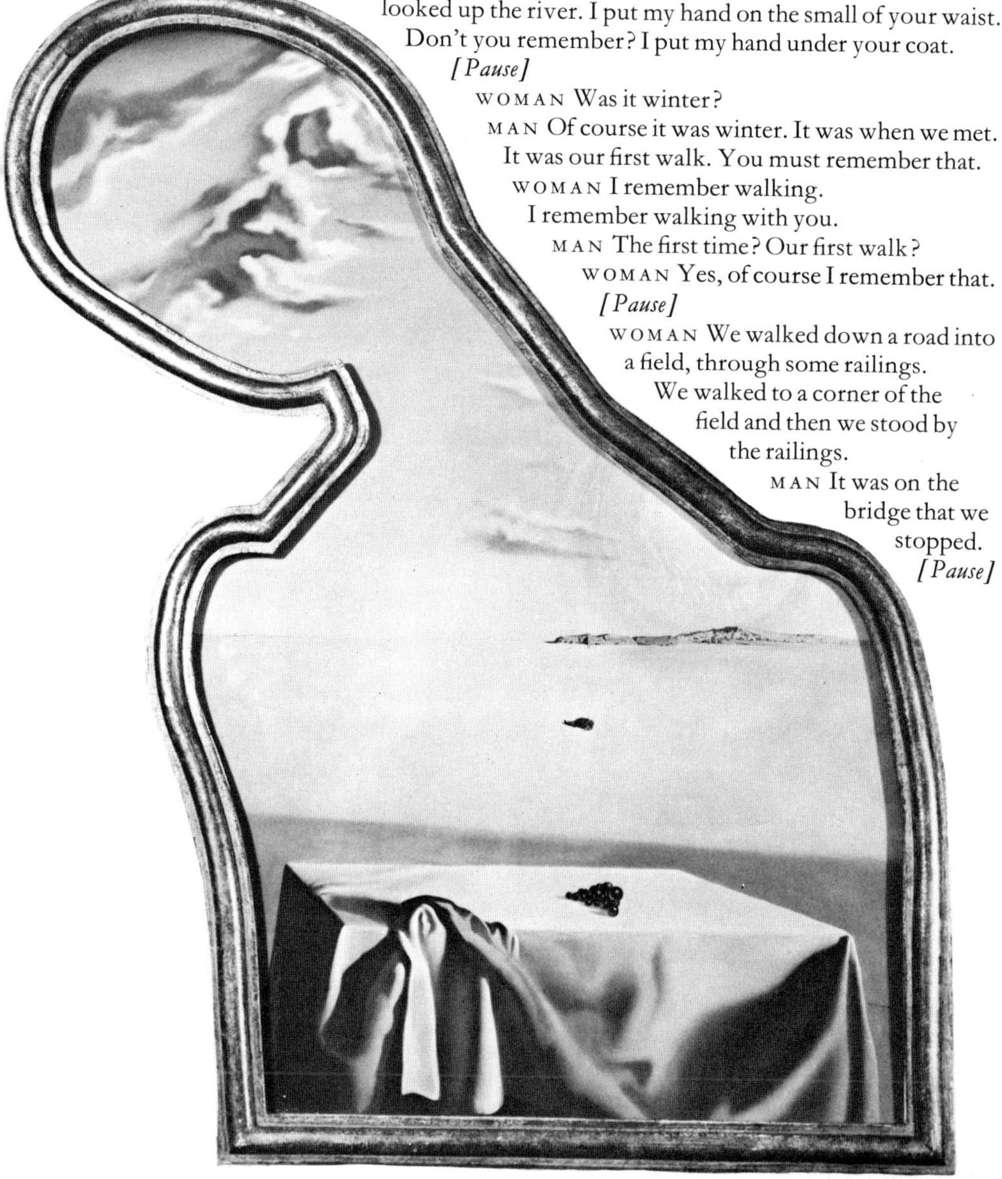

WOMAN That was someone else.

MAN Rubbish.

WOMAN That was another girl.

MAN It was years ago. You've forgotten.

[Pause]

MAN I remember the light on the water.

WOMAN You took my face in your hands, standing by the railings. You were very gentle, you were very caring. You cared. Your eyes searched my face. I wondered who you were. I wondered what you thought. I wondered what you would do.

MAN You agree we met at a party. You agree with that?

WOMAN What was that?

MAN What?

WOMAN I thought I heard a child crying.

MAN There was no sound.

WOMAN I thought it was a child, crying, waking up.

MAN The house is silent.

[Pause]

It's very late. We're sitting here. We should be in bed. I have to be up early. I have things to do. Why do you argue?

WOMAN I don't. I'm not. I'm willing to go to bed. I have things to do. I have to be up in the morning.

[Pause]

MAN A man called Doughty gave the party. You knew him. I had met him. I knew his wife. I met you there. You were standing by the window. I smiled at you, and to my surprise you smiled back. You liked me. I was amazed. You found me attractive. Later you told me. You liked my eyes.

WOMAN You liked mine.

[Pause]

WOMAN You touched my hand. You asked me who I was, and what I was, and whether I was aware that you were touching my hand, that your fingers were touching mine, that your fingers were moving up and down between mine.

MAN No. We stopped on a bridge. I stood behind you. I put my hand under your coat, on to your waist. You felt my hand on you.

[Pause]

WOMAN We had been to a party. Given by the Doughtys. You had known his wife. She looked at you dearly, as if to say you were her dear. She seemed to love you. I didn't. I didn't know you. They had a lovely house. By a river. I went to collect my coat, leaving you waiting for me. You had offered to escort me. I thought you were quite courtly, quite courteous, pleasantly mannered, quite caring. I slipped my coat on and looked out of the window, knowing you were waiting. I looked down over the garden to the river, and saw the lamplight on the water. Then I joined you and we walked down the road through railings into a field, must have been some kind of park. Later we found your car. You drove me.

[Pause]

MAN I touched your breasts.

WOMAN Where?

MAN On the bridge. I felt your breasts.

WOMAN Really?

MAN Standing behind you.

WOMAN I wondered whether you would, whether you wanted to, whether you would.

MAN Yes.

WOMAN I wondered how you would go about it, whether you wanted to, sufficiently.

MAN I put my hands under your sweater, I undid your brassière, I felt your breasts.

WOMAN Another night perhaps. Another girl.

MAN You don't remember my fingers on your skin?

WOMAN Were they in your hands? My breasts? Fully in your hands?

MAN You don't remember my hands on your skin?

[Pause]

WOMAN Standing behind me?

MAN Yes.

WOMAN But my back was against railings. I felt the railings . . . behind me. You were facing me. I was looking into your eyes. My coat was closed. It was cold.

MAN I undid your coat.

WOMAN It was very late. Chilly.

MAN And then we left the bridge and we walked down the towpath and we came to a rubbish-dump.

WOMAN And you had me and you told me you had fallen in love with me, and you said you would take care of me always, and you told me my voice and my eyes, my thighs, my breasts, were incomparable, and that you would adore me always.

MAN Yes I did.

WOMAN And you do adore me always.

MAN Yes I do.

WOMAN And then we had children and we sat and talked and you remembered women on bridges and towpaths and rubbish-dumps.

MAN And you remembered your bottom against railings and men holding your hands and men looking into your eyes.

WOMAN And talking to me softly.

MAN And your soft voice. Talking to them softly at night.

WOMAN And they said I will adore you always.

MAN Saying I will adore you always.

Harold Pinter

Modified Man

Work on a 'muscular system' which will outdo human muscles is already in hand. Under development at Cornell Aeronautical Laboratory, Buffalo, for the US Navy and Air Force is a 'man-amplifier'. Like a lobster, which carries its skeleton outside its flesh, not inside as we do, the amplified man wears a steel 'exoskeleton' powered by hydraulic motors instead of muscles. Inside it he wears a light framework equipped with sensors which sense his every movement and cause the exoskeleton to repeat or follow it instantaneously. Preliminary designs called for the man-amplifier to be able to support a load of 1000 lb (half a ton) on either hand. Eventually, of course, such amplified men will be able to cope with much greater loads: to lift an automobile with one hand will be child's play.

Unfortunately, most of the power sources currently available (compressed gases, electric motors, etc.) rely on rapid rotatory movement and develop very little power at low speeds. Muscles, in contrast, exert a considerable effort relatively slowly and in a straight line. The hydraulic units employed for the prototype man-amplifier proved awkwardly bulky. But at the Weizmann Institute of Science in Israel, artificial muscles, which contract as real muscles do, are under development, and something on these lines will no doubt prove the answer for the powered exoskeleton, and also for the prosthetic arms now being designed for amputees.

This sort of development has led some prophets to foresee the emergence of a new relationship between man and machines, a relationship in which the two become so intermixed as to be virtually indistinguishable. The word 'cyborg' (an abbreviation of cybernetic organism) has been coined for such hybrids. The essential difference between them is two-way. The machine not only receives instructions from the man but also informs the man of the conditions it is encountering, just as his own hands or feet do.

Ralph S. Mosher, of General Electric, prefers to speak of the CAM concept, for Cybernetic Anthropomorphic Machines, and for this company he built 'Handyman': two arms and hands which repeat on a larger and more powerful scale anything that their master does with his arms and hands. Each hand has ten independent motions, but the key feature is that the mechanical muscles feed back to the operator the resistances they encounter. A robot without this 'force feedback' feature, trying to open a door, would probably tear the handle off. To open a door, one must let one's hand follow the arc of the door handle. One robot handler (made by another company), which lacked this device, attempted to punch a button on the wall and pushed the wall down. 'Handyman' can twirl a skipping rope; in doing this you have to sense from the varying pull on the rope the right instant to put more energy into it, so that a robot without feedback could not do this.

When I went to visit Dr Mosher, I saw 'Handyman' pick up a small child and put her down again. The non-feedback type of handler might have crushed her or sent her through the roof.

Inspired by the success of 'Handyman', General Electric are building for the US Army a 'pedipulator' or walker, which will enable its wearer to take giant strides across country, as if on stilt-long legs. But unlike stilts, his metal legs will have knee and ankle joints, and will convey to him information about his balance. For the future, they see a combination of these devices, with which a man will be able not only to walk and grasp objects, but to swim rivers or swing from branch to branch. Clearly these are not machines – they only function when a man is functioning – they are man-amplifiers.

In the ordinary way it seems unlikely that men will want to maintain a relationship with these devices longer than is necessary. But in the alien conditions of another planet, they may need to live with them for weeks. To put a man in a clumsy and weighty space-suit and then ask him to climb into a vehicle may prove less sensible than to make his space-suit his vehicle also. (On the moon, with its weak gravitational force, the weight of space-suits and oxygen equipment is not so important, but on large planets they could become too heavy for a man to move in.) With his customary prescience, H. G. Wells foresaw this development; in *The War of the Worlds* the Martians are spider-like creatures which spend almost all their time in three-legged pedipulators.

The second of the developments which contribute to the cyborg concept is the growing use of mechanical prostheses. As long as artificial kidneys and heart-lung machines are so bulky they must remain external to the body: but they could be built into man-amplifiers, thus restoring to the wearer his lost mobility. The partially paralysed patient could also be given mobility and a wider range of activities by such a procedure.

At the same time, the past few years have seen the development of the first artificial arms controlled by currents from the wearer's muscles. The wearer simply thinks of raising his arm, and up the artificial arm goes. When the original limb is amputated high up, so that the operating muscles are removed as well, the signal can be taken from other muscles, so that the wearer may have to think of shrugging his shoulders in order to raise his arms, but this the brain is quite good at doing. As with the muscle-amplifier, the limiting factor on these 'myoelectric' prostheses, at present, is lack of a really satisfactory power source. Bottles of liquefied gas are chiefly used, which are on the heavy side, and last only a few hours. But the storage of power is being steadily improved, and it is unlikely this problem will remain unsolved for long.

Put these two concepts together – the CAM and myoelectric control – and we can picture a man embedded in a machine which does what he

wants as soon as he thinks about it, without any muscular intervention on his part. The machine becomes, in a more literal sense than ever before, an extension of man. Here, still more, lies hope for the paralytic patient and it is reasonable to expect that one day paraplegics and others, if they can't be cured, will permanently inhabit a sort of metal body.

But this argument can be taken to a still more extraordinary stage. The brain itself (which can now be maintained outside the body) could be placed in such a metal body, which would be equipped with the necessary devices for perfusing it with blood, lymph and so on, and could then live indefinitely, until overtaken by its own senility. This we might christen 'total prosthesis'. While such a development may well be a century or more in the future, it is not to be dismissed as pure fantasy. It will certainly raise ethical, not to mention social, problems. Presumably it would be murder to refuse such a total prosthesis to anyone demanding it, and it would be suicide not to demand it. Society would therefore find itself faced, in a much more specific way than is now the case with dialysis machines, with an obligation which must certainly prove exceedingly costly.

A variant on this pattern can be foreseen in the current development, for space purposes, of 'slaves' or robot doubles. The idea, advanced by William E. Bradley of the Institute of Defense Analyses in Washington, is simply to take the robot handler just described and introduce a radio link between it and the operator. The radio link would carry sound and television signals, instructions from the operator to the slave and force feedback from the slave to the operator. In this way, an astronaut could sit within his spacecraft, while his slave went out into space to make a repair or to link up equipment – the advantage being that the slave requires no oxygen supply, heating or other maintenance while there, and is impervious to radiation, while danger to the astronaut is minimized. Equally, slaves could be sent out on the surface of the moon; if one dropped into a crevasse, it could be replaced by another. To make life more difficult, Bradley has named his proposed slave a 'telefactor'.

Owing to the time lag in signals, it would not be really practicable to send such slaves to the moon and control them from earth, but it would be possible to control aircraft or spacecraft in orbital flight in this way, or to control slaves on the moon from a spacecraft in moon orbit. Even on the earth, such slaves would be particularly useful in radiation fields which would be damaging or lethal to man, and some of the development work on them has been financed for this reason.

Applying this concept to the medical and civil situations we have been envisaging, we can see that, before it becomes possible to put a brain in a fully mobile body, it should be possible to provide it with a slave. The brain would then repose in sterilized surroundings, where it could be perfused by apparatus which might still be bulky, and could be watched over by medical attendants continuously, while its slave went to board-meetings, played chess or dined with friends, continuously relaying the appropriate stimuli back to its owner, and responding to his commands. (It is to be hoped that interference-free radio channels will be available by this time!)

It seems unlikely that the tremendous technological effort involved in such a feat would be made available in the lifetime of anyone now living, except perhaps in one circumstance. It may not be quite out of the question that a paranoid dictator, finding himself afflicted by a slowly developing but mortal disease such as cancer, or simply by old age, should attempt to prolong his domination by such methods. I do not suggest that it would happen today: the time required to develop the equipment would be longer than a man in such a position could afford to wait. But in fifty years, when the technologies are fully developed, when slave-handlers have been perfected for space purposes and when ectopic brain maintenance is a commonplace, the final step of bringing them all together need not take very long.

At this point, the question, raised earlier, of the right to die, may raise its head. The ectopic brain (to coin a phrase, for we have no word at present for such a situation) of the paranoid dictator may find life in these conditions unbearable and regret his decision. But his aides may think his continued existence politically indispensable – as is often held to be the case in wartime – and decline to cut off the juices which maintain his existence, a situation of classic irony.

There is also a third development which has contributed to the cyborg concept – the development of the computer. Man and machine are here developing what must be called an intellectual relationship, at present best seen in the teaching-machine approach. Computers have been used to teach medical students diagnosis, putting to them the symptoms and commenting on their replies and further questions just as a human teacher would. At present such dialogues take place through a typewriter keyboard, the student's observations being typed in, and the machine printing out its answers.

Within a quarter of a century, however, we shall see the machine listen to spoken questions and enunciate its replies.

This aspect must also be placed in conjunction with those previously outlined. The computer, in principle, can also be given slave extensions, or placed in metal pedipulating bodies. When this occurs, we have the robot of Čapek's imagination. But the slave-equipped robot will come long before the fully mobile one, and computer-controlled manipulators already exist in the laboratory stage.

Finally, we can add to this series of extrapolations the converse of the notion of placing mechanical parts in a living body viz. the placing of living parts in a mechanical body. The suggestion that brains should be placed in CAMS is one instance; but it is not inconceivable that a human arm, or at any rate an ape's or a monkey's, could be coupled to a computer. (An ear or eye might be more difficult.) In short, a complex marriage seems to be taking place between man and machine. The science-fiction writer Isaac Asimov has foretold the establishment of a new race of man-machine hybrids; one day it may become impossible to tell whether one is talking to a mechanized human being or a humanized machine. Or even which one is oneself.

Gordon Rattray Taylor *The Biological Time Bomb*

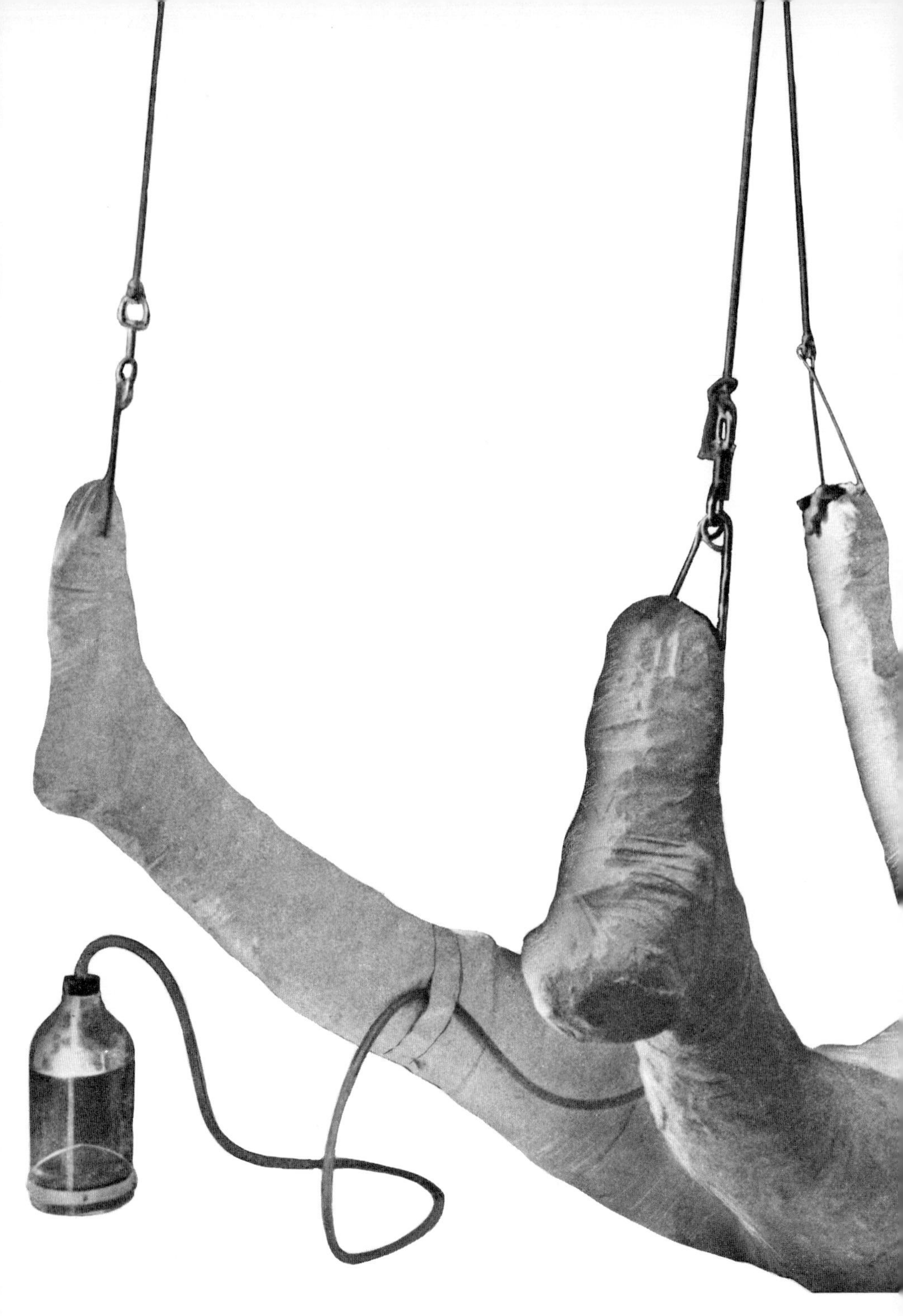

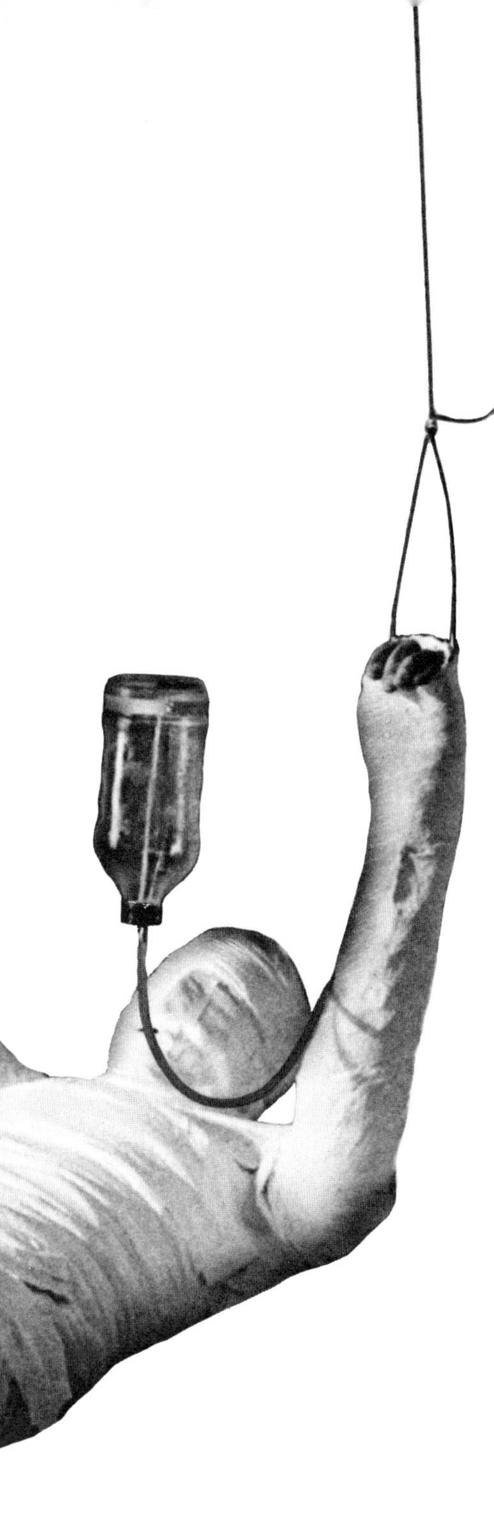

The Soldier in White

The soldier in white was constructed entirely of gauze, plaster and a thermometer, and the thermometer was merely an adornment left balanced in the empty dark hole in the bandages over his mouth early each morning and late each afternoon by Nurse Cramer and Nurse Duckett right up to the afternoon Nurse Cramer read the thermometer and discovered he was dead. Now that Yossarian looked back, it seemed that Nurse Cramer, rather than the talkative Texan, had murdered the soldier in white; if she had not read the thermometer and reported what she had found, the soldier in white might still be lying there alive exactly as he had been lying there all along, encased from head to toe in plaster and gauze with both strange, rigid legs elevated from the hips and both strange arms strung up perpendicularly, all four bulky limbs in casts, all four strange, useless limbs hoisted up in the air by taut wire cables and fantastically long lead weights suspended darkly above him. Lying there that way might not have been much of a life, but it was all the life he had, and the decision to terminate it, Yossarian felt, should hardly have been Nurse Cramer's.

The soldier in white was like an unrolled bandage with a hole in it or like a broken block of stone in a harbour with a crooked zinc pipe jutting out. The other patients in the ward, all but the Texan, shrank from him with a tenderhearted aversion from the moment they set eyes on him the morning after the night he had been sneaked in. They gathered soberly in the farthest recess of the ward and gossiped about him in malicious, offended undertones, rebelling against his presence as a ghastly imposition and resenting him malevolently for the nauseating truth of which he was bright reminder. They shared a common dread that he would begin moaning.

'I don't know what I'll do if he does begin moaning,' the dashing young fighter pilot with the golden moustache had grieved forlornly. 'It means he'll moan during the night, too, because he won't be able to tell time.'

No sound at all came from the soldier in white all the time he was here. The ragged round hole over his mouth was deep and jet black and showed no sign of lip, teeth, palate or tongue. The only one who ever came close enough to look was the affable Texan, who came close enough several times a day to chat with him about more votes for the decent folk, opening each conversation with the same unvarying greeting: 'What do you say, fella? How you coming along?' The rest of the men avoided them both in their regulation maroon corduroy bathrobes and unravelling flannel pyjamas, wondering gloomily who the soldier in white was, why he was there and what he was really like inside.

'He's all right, I tell you,' the Texan would report back to them encouragingly after each of his social visits. 'Deep down inside he's really a regular guy. He's just feeling a little shy and insecure now because he doesn't know anybody here and can't talk. Why don't you all just step right up to him and introduce yourselves? He won't hurt you.'

'What the goddam hell are you talking about?' Dunbar demanded. 'Does he even know what you're talking about?'

'Sure he knows what I'm talking about. He's not stupid. There ain't nothing wrong with him.'

'Can he hear you?'

'Well, I don't know if he can hear me or not, but I'm sure he knows what I'm talking about.'

'Does that hole over his mouth ever move?'

'Now, what kind of a crazy question is that?' the Texan asked uneasily.

'How can you tell if he's breathing if it never moves?'

'How can you tell it's a he?'

'Does he have pads over his eyes underneath that bandage over his face?'

'Does he ever wiggle his toes or move the tips of his fingers?'

The Texan backed away in mounting confusion. 'Now, what kind of a crazy question is that? You fellas must all be crazy or something. Why don't you just walk right up to him and get acquainted? He's a real nice guy, I tell you.'

The soldier in white was more like a stuffed and sterilized mummy than a real nice guy. Nurse Duckett and Nurse Cramer kept him spick-and-span. They brushed his bandages often with a whiskbroom and scrubbed the plaster casts on his arms, legs, shoulders, chest and pelvis with soapy water. Working with a round tin of metal polish, they waxed a dim gloss on the dull zinc pipe rising from the cement on his groin. With damp dish towels they wiped the dust several times a day from the slim black rubber tubes leading in and out of him to the two large stoppered jars, one of them, hanging on a post beside his bed, dripping fluid into his arm constantly through a slit in the bandages while the other, almost out of sight on the floor, drained the fluid away through the zinc pipe rising from his groin. Both young nurses polished the glass jars unceasingly. They were proud of their work. The more solicitous of the two was Nurse Cramer, a shapely, pretty, sexless girl with a wholesome unattractive face. Nurse Cramer had a cute nose and a radiant blooming complexion dotted with fetching sprays of adorable freckles that Yossarian detested. She was touched very deeply by the soldier in white. Her virtuous, pale-blue, saucerlike eyes flooded with leviathan tears on unexpected occasions and made Yossarian mad.

'How the hell do you know he's even in there?' he asked her.

'Don't you dare talk to me that way!' she replied indignantly.

'Well, how do you? You don't even know if it's really him.'

'Who?'

'Whoever's supposed to be in all those bandages. You might really be weeping for somebody else. How do you know he's even alive?'

'What a terrible thing to say!' Nurse Cramer exclaimed. 'Now, you get right into bed and stop making jokes about him.'

'I'm not making jokes. Anybody might be in there. For all we know it might be Mudd.'

'What are you talking about?' Nurse Cramer pleaded with him in a quavering voice.

'Maybe that's where the dead man is.'

'What dead man?'

'I've got a dead man in my tent that nobody can throw out. His name is Mudd.'

Nurse Cramer's face blanched and she turned to Dunbar desperately for aid. 'Make him stop saying things like that,' she begged.

'Maybe there's no one inside,' Dunbar suggested helpfully. 'Maybe they just sent the bandages here for a joke.'

She stepped away from Dunbar in alarm. 'You're crazy,' she cried, glancing about imploringly. 'You're both crazy.'

Nurse Duckett showed up then and chased them all back to their own beds while Nurse Cramer changed the stoppered jars for the soldier in white. Changing the jars for the soldier in white was no trouble at all, since the same clear fluid was dripped back inside him over and over again with no apparent loss. When the jar feeding the inside of his elbow was just about empty, the jar on the floor was just about full, and the two were simply uncoupled from their respective hoses and reversed quickly so the liquid could be dripped right back into him. Changing the jars was no trouble to anyone but the men who watched them changed every hour or so and were baffled by the procedure.

'Why can't they hook the two jars up to each other and eliminate the middleman?' the artillery captain with whom Yossarian had stopped playing chess inquired. 'What the hell do they need him for?'

'I wonder what he did to deserve it,' the warrant officer with malaria and a mosquito bite on his ass lamented after Nurse Cramer had read her thermometer and discovered that the soldier in white was dead.

'He went to war,' the fighter pilot with the golden moustache surmised.

'We all went to war,' Dunbar countered.

Joseph Heller *Catch-22*

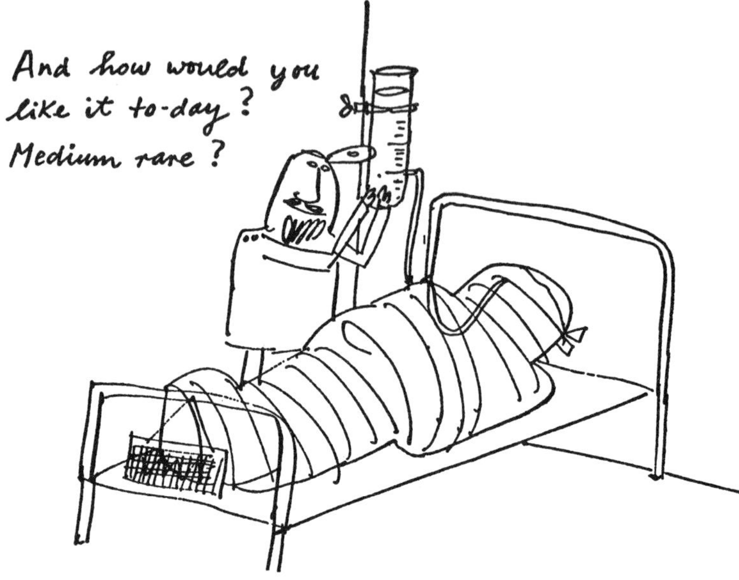

Directions to the Armourer

All right, armourer,
Make me a sword –
Not too sharp,
A bit hard to draw,
And of cardboard, preferably.
On second thought, stick
An eraser on the handle.
Somehow I always
Clobber the wrong guy.

Make me a shield with
Easy-to-change
Insignia. I'm often
A little vague
As to which side I'm on,
What battle I'm in.
And listen, make it
A trifle flimsy,
Not too hard to pierce.
I'm not absolutely sure
I want to win.

Make the armour itself
As tough as possible,
But on a reverse
Principle: don't
Worry about its
Saving my hide;
Just fix it to give me
Some sort of protection –
Any sort of protection –
From a possible enemy
Inside.

Elder Olson

I am Well, Who are You?

It is more than twenty years now since the end of the war; but for many of the war generation the ordeals still reverberate in the mind. In this long and moving account of the effects of a Japanese prisoner-of-war camp, David Piper (now Director of the National Portrait Gallery and Slade Professor of Fine Arts) describes the continuing effects of the limbo of 'not being all there', and the lingering doubts about one's own identity.

I sat in a long low bamboo hut on one of a long row of bamboo beds; the hut was full of a diffused light, but clear and still golden, from the bright September sunlight beyond the low eaves outside. It was still as calm water, for all the roar of the planes above; on each bed a figure sat or lay in a solid and closed patience, waiting. The air was a little

sweet-sour with the familiar odour of more than two or three gathered together in the grip of dysentery.

As all of us, I too was waiting. As all of us, I was at this stage thinnish, six foot one inch, weighing not more than between ninety and a hundred pounds; I wore a pair of briefs made from an old flour sack (they had a stencilled crowing cock in red on the right buttock – or rather where the buttock used to be in meatier days – and some Chinese ideograms on the left).

The man on the next bed sat facing me, equally thin, except that his belly was enormously swollen with beriberi. He wore nothing at all except a little metal nozzle screwed into the belly, and through this the extraneous fluid that his disease had built up in his tissue peed steadily in a limpish arc down into a tin container on the floor between his open legs. Its splashing was mostly not audible, for over the roofs of the bamboo huts the American B-29s were coming in very low, one after the other in bursting crescendo, opening their huge silver bellies, too, and dropping their loads.

I waited in a state of suspended disbelief, a condition that had lasted some days now, since the Japanese had announced that the war was over. Thus I knew in theory that the war *was* over, that in a matter of days, hours even, we would be taken off the island of Formosa where we had been prisoners for three years; I knew also that the bombers were unloading not bombs, but huge shining metal cylinders, packed with food and floating down on parachutes, for us. Nevertheless instinct expected, almost demanded, bombs; we had been bombed by B-29s before, as we had been machine-gunned by their dancing consorts, the twin-tailed fighters.

Then the passage of another one overhead was followed by an odd crashing noise, rather muffled, but provoking in the distance a sudden ragged clamour of panic voices. Men came running past the hut, shouting to take cover. The nozzle in my companion's stomach skipped slightly and then flowed evenly on. In the process of limbering up painfully to get under my bed, I caught his eye, and he shrugged slightly and the nozzle twitched again. I stopped getting under my bed, and looked instead out of the hut into the radiant September morning. No one was moving there now, and the bombers were still coming on and over and over. When they had finished, movement began again outside, loudly querulous in the silence after the planes; everyone seemed to be arguing and swearing. The nozzle had ceased to flow, though my companion's great paunch seemed none the smaller for what it had lost.

Some men went past at a run, with empty stretchers. 'Accident,' said my companion, and brooded.

A tall gaunt man went past in a slow, careful strut of some majesty. He wore a G-string and his belly seemed almost as big, though more solid, as that of the man on the next bed; he walked his belly in front of himself as if it were a perambulator full of a very rare and royal baby.

'Sergeant Oakes,' said my companion. 'Ate eighty-seven eggs last night. For a bet.'

He moved restlessly, and shouted. 'George! Com'n undo me, for Christ sake!'

A figure came towards us from the door at the end of the hut.

'Silly,' said my companion, brooding again and referring to Sergeant Oakes. 'Do himself a damage.'

George arrived; he was an orderly. He detached the nozzle, swabbed the distended skin, patched it, and manoeuvred the lop-sided torso up and down into a lying position on the bed. He was saying that the parachutes on two of the food canisters had failed to open. 'Went thundering slap through the roof of a hut. Burst like a bloody bomb. two men copped it, and several hurt.'

The men who had been killed and wounded were not from the camp we have been in, and we didn't know them.

The hulk on the next bed had closed his eyes and was resting. 'Silly,' he said without opening his eyes. 'Getting killed. Three and half years you manage not to die, then get knocked off by a bloody great can of condensed milk dropped on you in loving kindness.'

He breathed heavily, and the jelly of his stomach wobbled.

'Funny, really,' he said.

At that time, early September 1945, there were other bombs more in the news. We were aware, as we waited in this central clearing camp in the north of Formosa for the Navy to come and take us away, that vital raids with extra-big bombs had been made on Hiroshima and Nagasaki, and that an incomprehensible number had been killed in those raids. That these bombs were not just bigger, but of an entirely different order, we were not as yet aware. Probably the knowledge at this point that mankind was now able to obliterate itself in a matter of hours or even minutes, would not have had much impact on us. For us, the result of the bomb was rebirth. If we had known the cost of our release it would doubtless have seemed no more than our due, and overdue at that. Had the war gone on, our chances of remaining alive would have diminished ever more rapidly with each week that passed, and some of us were aware of the alternative plans the Japanese had prepared for us in the event of an armed invasion of Formosa by the Allies; either plan would have meant our inevitable liquidation, though one plan, of simple massacre, would have been more abrupt than the other.

For what we had survived, limbo three and a half years long, I can still find very few words. The cruelties of the Japanese camps are notorious and only too well documented. In any case the day-to-day brutality rested on a certain logic which most prisoners came to comprehend; the Japanese army backed its own normal discipline with blows, and like all other armies had its chain of command; thus a blow given by an officer to an NCO would be passed on to the private, lower than whom was only the prisoner of war, who consequently always collected the last, though generally by no means least, blow. As elsewhere, the Japanese camps in Formosa saw some outbreaks of apparently insane berserk violence; one does not because one cannot forget things like the systematic beating up of patients in the hospital huts. But in Formosa we were from that aspect relatively fortunate, and suffered nothing comparable in scale with the horrors of the Burma railway or the Java death marches.

For a decade after the war I was haunted by the need to formulate, precipitate the essential character and significance of our prison existence, and frustrated by the apparent impossiblity of translating it into a form comprehensive to anyone who had not shared it. Only in 1955 was I released from this need, when I saw Beckett's *Waiting for Godot*. That play for me was a near-perfect statement of the prisoner's condition of suspension in stagnant time, and I recognized it with profound gratitude. It deals of course in rather general terms, and does not touch upon some specific facets of my own experience, especially hunger, and in this the Formosan experience was as bad and at times probably worse than in any other camps. Acute hunger, stretched over years, is beyond the normal scope of Europeans and Americans. In practice, it becomes quite quickly paramount; it strips the body to a bleak anatomy, and dissolves mind and spirit within one ravenous physical appetite. Below a certain subsistence level, other considerations vanish – for three and a half years, for example, the needs of sex were nil. On the other hand, the urgency of hunger was the essential governor of survival, its insistent concentration surely the reason why so few prisoners went mad. Only when it faded could despair overwhelm fatally; known in all Far Eastern prison camps was that stage in a prisoner's illness when hunger failed; then the man would turn his face to the wall, and simply surrender life, and die – not necessarily for pathological reasons, but because he had no longer any incentive to live. But twenty years later, I can no longer feel, even remember, this state of being hungry, of living as hunger.

I still have my rice bowl, three and a half inches across, two and a half inches high; at bad times this, filled with boiled rice three times a day, was our total food ration. I use it as an ashtray.

We had then for years waited for Godot. Now many of us were dazed, distracted by inexpressible elations, but also by new fears. We had entered into our waiting through catastrophe and defeat; we had become attuned to perpetual catastrophe and yet now we would be free. No one knew how Godot would reveal himself; what the face of freedom would prove – whether it would even be bearable. For we had become conditioned by captivity, and sickly secure in it. One might die, one might be beaten up by one's captors or bombed by one's allies, but there was nothing whatsoever one could do about it; there were no decisions to take. Now decisions would be thrust upon us.

So we went, timorous and excited, out into freedom: on stretchers into British destroyers and thence into the US flat-top *Santeo*, which had been miraculously transformed into a hospital ship. We went with our earthly possessions clutched to us: pants made of flour bags, a safety-razor blade that had already served eighteen months, sheaves of rough paper covered with lovingly indited imaginary menus, empty tins for putting things in; and they threw most of these into the Pacific. They dunked us in antiseptic and shaved every hair off our bodies and threw the hair in the sea. They fed us twenty-four hours a day on a soft diet scientifically calculated not to distress our starved gut; they treated us with endless kindness, amazement and incomprehension. How could they comprehend? How could they understand the value beyond pearls that an empty coffee tin for putting things in, should things turn up, could have for us? We could not comprehend them – even their vocabulary bristling with words we had never heard, words as simple as 'jeep'. They were saturated and radiant with victory, a victory to which we had contributed nothing and of which we knew very little – of the war in Europe almost nothing. They were radiantly confident in sheer health, and we went among them as shaven skeletons with distended pot stomachs; we were paupers and like paupers we were envious, mentally stripping the rich flesh from our rescuers' bodies, to reduce them to our own size, to see what they would look like thin. They smelled strange, at once affluent and gross, and from this we deduced that to them we stank of prison and defeat and disease. Politely they asked us what it had been like, and we could not tell them; when we tried to tell them, they changed the subject soon enough, and soon too we learned not to try.

Yet there was, of course, above all this a huge exhilaration, also inexpressible. Tears of sheer frustration and wonder. On the first morning out from Formosa, the clouds lifted, and the rainbows thrown by the sun in the spray of the carrier's bow wave for the moment were enough for pure happiness. The world opened out in the immense marine sky; eyes flew drunken to the horizon, and it seemed one had to haul them back in.

Near Manila we sighted another aircraft carrier; it stood a mile or so off us; from its deck they were pushing obsolete aircraft into the sea as from ours they had jettisoned our empty tins. Then it was Manila harbour and we swarmed excitedly; a launch came alongside, and one of the uniforms coming aboard had skirts. In company with at least half my prison mates, I withdrew in panic from exposure to woman. We were landed, and went into another camp. Material goods fell upon us from heaven. We dressed in American uniforms, drank beer cautiously, chain-smoked and went in and out of the ever-open cafeteria, until there came a point when I was sitting there with a piled-up tray in front of me unable to touch it. All my instincts, conditioned by the habit of hunger, letched for it, but my clogged stomach could no longer encompass it. Again the frustrated tears came to my eyes. I lived in a round tent from which on wavering legs I made cautious, controlled, dangerous forays into the unknown of a hundred yards away, returning from each one exhausted, damp with sweat, as if after a jungle patrol.

I was in the Manila transit camp two weeks, and in that time the tentacles of the past came reaching out from the distance. A cable from my parents in England. Then one from the girl I had left behind me, in the London blitz of December 1940, five years ago. She was in

Burma, in Rangoon; meet me, she wired, in India, at Darjeeling. For a day I summoned strength and resolution in my tent, chain-smoking cigars, and then made a desperate miles-long sortie, to the airfield. American planes were leaving direct for Calcutta; she was but hours from me. I explained my urgency, in confusion, my knees buckling. The officials were sympathetic but firm. If I did not have the dollars for the fare I could not go; last week, they said thoughtfully, I could have gone free, but now Lend-Lease was finished. I had no money at all; defeated, I watched the plane, half-empty, climb up into the dusk, and drifted back through the night to my safe tent, perhaps half-relieved. Not yet; for after all, who was she, whom I had known five years ago, a war ago, in another life?

We began again to travel, not towards India but in the opposite direction, in another flat-top across the huge purple swell of the Pacific to Vancouver. A British ship this time, the crew all kind and remote and uncomprehending. The ship's captain, a Royal Navy officer, wished to hold a daily muster parade of his guests; we attended unpunctually in strange attire, often (as it was still very warm) in utmost undress, bringing our deck chairs and our books and our poker dice. On the bridge, the captain gazed down on the motley crowd and mantled with anger; he explained to me his wish for the ex-prisoners to dress properly, to fall in and drill by the right, and to answer their names. I said they would be happy to comply with his last wish, but not with the other two. I tried to explain to the captain that a habit of three and a half years' standing of mutely insolent non-cooperation with all authority was not lightly cast off, and the captain swelled to what seemed a dangerous pitch of red-turkey fury and I left the bridge and went back to my bunk and my book.

Vancouver was busy bustling, without a scar of war; the people were obscenely fat and confident, and I was a ghost among them. I stayed with a rich man who had once known my father. A butler with a budgerigar perched on his left shoulder slid noiselessly into the bathroom, where I lay in the deep hot water, bearing large whiskies clanging with ice. For ten days I was Cinderella, and left equipped with a wristwatch, a civilian suit, and dress lengths for my mother and my girl. We pierced Canada by train from west to east; at Calgary Station there was a triumphant greeting from the local band of girl pipers; at seven o'clock in the morning we were all heroes, and I survived the bear hug of the drum majorette with ice-blue thighs before breakfast at some degrees below zero. We dipped south to New York. My nervous assault on Times Square was routed by an intolerable counter-assault, a barrage of noise and lights and people and people. I dived for the subway, and back to the Transit Camp where soft-spoken, infinitely patient welfare workers kitted me out further with bedroom slippers, pyjamas, a flannelette dressing gown and a chunky sweater knitted for me, according to the label, by the women of Chile. Then we all got on to the *Queen Mary* and, complaining incessantly about the food, sailed home. The green banks of the Solent closed in on me like brakes, and it was all over; it had taken me five years to do it, but I had completed the circuit of the world.

In the railway station at Bristol: my father. He seemed shrunk in his pre-war overcoat, and grey now. We are not a talking family, but we shook hands and he said it was good to see me and how was I. I subdued an overpowering desire to get back in the train, and said I was fine, thank you. We got into the pre-war car; the steering wheel had the cloth cover, meticulously sewn on by mother, that it had had when I left; my father drove as always, precisely and attentively, but on this occasion had some uncharacteristic trouble with the gears. There was the modest house I had been brought up in; there was my mother, she too somewhat shrunk and in a shadow of apprehensive sadness that was unfamiliar. It was all there, the house, the furniture, my own old room. It was home; I had last seen it when I was twenty-two and now I was twenty-seven, and took up habitation in it as a ghost, moving slowly and very carefully lest I should walk through it all.

They said I had beaten the girl from Rangoon home by a few days, hours even; she was bustling back from Burma and India the other way. Confrontation loomed. I had known her, loved her, so I thought, for a little more than a year in 1939–40. For five years I had carried her image with me, vital to me, yet an image that must inevitably through the years and the hunger have frozen into a bloodless asexual icon, dehydrated pin-up or a St Christopher badge such as a traveller wears round his neck for luck and prayer. As this image had grown thus gradually simplified and idealized, distorted from reality, in me, so she in turn must have been growing away from it in directions of which I had no inkling, through the five years of her own war. The possibility of even merest superficial recognition seemed remote – on either side. I looked at my new self in the mirror, and it looked back no longer thin, for in three months of compulsive eating I had doubled my weight and dwelled now in an envelope of soft, insipid fat; my hair had attained a stubble height. If I wished to go out of the house I had to summon up courage to do so for half an hour beforehand; the telephone terrified me, and the prospect of meeting either people I had known before or new people was torment. Physically I was actively repellent, etiolated, a snail that had foolishly strayed out without its shell. I did not seem a working proposition for any girl.

I was lying on the floor, trying to make a newspaper make sense, when I heard her come. A voice in the hall that shrivelled me. I lay paralysed; the door opened and shut again behind her and I stared at the newsprint. Then I looked quickly and furtively. She was gorgeous, her hair the colour and shine of autumn beech woods, and she all honey below, but wild, and sparkling. She fell all over me, and I grabbed all of her, body, legs, arms; hair, face and mouth. She smelt like harvest corn at evening, laced thoughtfully with the finest scent of Paris; on her thigh the suspender went *boing*. She was good and solid and elastic, and I knew that I knew nothing whatsoever about her except that she was good and solid and elastic and we were working about the floor like all-in wrestlers, and that it would all be all right; it was real.

That evening we talked politely to my prospective father-in-law over long-distance telephone to Edinburgh. In the distant North he did not seem to hear very well, and his faint voice wanted to know what the hurry was, but he had no serious objections. So we got married and down along five honeymoons, one after the other, I fell in love and we lived happily ever after.

It is all twenty years ago. We have been lucky, thus far. At the worst times as prisoner, I would make Faust-like pacts with some unnamed devil or divinity: 'Just let me out of here and give me ten years. Ten years of life will do.' I have had twenty. My eldest daughter is eighteen, going up to Cambridge this autumn; I met her mother at Cambridge when she was eighteen. Twenty years after 1918, when I was first born, and the First World War ended, brought me to 1938 and Munich. Now it is the same span of years since 1945 and the end of the Second World War; there have been the Cold War, Korea, Suez, Cuba, Cyprus, Algeria; now Vietnam. This was the week the Press reported the murder of Joseph Grainger, a US aid official, in Vietnam; captured by the Vietcong, escaped after months, and then surprised by a patrol in jungle, washing mud off in a stream. 'It was nine o'clock in the morning. Mr Grainger refused to return into captivity. A man called Hai shot him, twice. They carried him to their village headquarters, and there, late that day, he died.'

It still goes on. It is not even always decently far away on the other side of the world. Not long ago, the house next door to ours in London changed hands, and one bright and calm morning I wandered after breakfast into our backyard to inspect the weeds that we grow so well, and suddenly my hair stood on end, and I could not breathe. In the garden next door stood a Japanese. Japanese-Hawaiian-American he proved subsequently to be, and a charmer, but for those first few seconds, as he stood there in a flowered shirt watering his garden and not even knowing I was there, he had me a prisoner again. But it is all only momentary, and from such shocks I revert carefully to my vegetable existence.

That existence, these last twenty years, has been far from admirable, apolitical, undevoted to the betterment of mankind. I am now forty, my hair thins and I smoke too much and do not pay proper attention to my clothes; I press upon the elderly, and thus am prone to tedious reminiscence. A doubtless congenital need for security, but certainly sharpened by an acquired prison mentality, led me to the Civil Service, with firmly assured conditions of employment and a pension smiling faintly in the far distance. I have been ultimately unmoved by public events, only reacting sharply when they threatened my private events; even to the Bomb I was ambivalent, for though it threatens my pension it had saved my life. My passions are private and ordinary. My wife; our children; art (I have been lucky again in that the British Civil Service embraces in its maternal scope the national museums and galleries, on one of which I work). My wife, our children are my life in flux, being and always becoming. Art, the expression of an immutable order within flux, becomes almost monthly a deeper necessity. These are enough. They are selfish concerns, perhaps even frivolous. I have squandered my own talents, again perhaps frivolously. I would like to make a true and perfectly built book, but I become more and more aware of the difficulties of writing truly and well; competitiveness fades, and I become more content rather to admire and rejoice in what others have made, and are making, superlatively. I have proved even an indifferent scholar, helpless as Canute before the insidious tides of error. I would like to create a gallery of pictures, in my job, that would bewitch all who came into it; the dream limps through thickets of resistant practical detail, and halts for months at a stretch before chasms full of no money.

Yet contentment keeps entering in; mostly I am happy, living in a beautiful if decrepit house on the banks of the Thames, going about the London that I love. And my vegetable state is always conditioned by one of the better inheritances of prison life: a sense of perpetual precariousness within security. For a little time after liberation this was a constant, electrifying sensation as if walking on a tightrope; each step vertigo in a glory of danger. So, often still, I am shaken with wonder at being alive.

If I am frivolous, I reflect only the greater frivolity of fate; leaves dance in the wind, but the wind is the greater idiot. War taught me the fickle lightness of life, as prison camps taught me the frail tenacity of survival. Excellent to know one is worthless and alive.

There are of course, to set against this, the recurring problems that range from the hauntingly petty (how to confront the telephone) to larger ones, such as the problem that has seemed especially insistent for my generation, the problem of identity. To know that one is one, if worthless. For me this comes irregularly though frequently to minor crisis, and for me it may be intensified because I see (looking back, it did not seem so at the time) my former fellow prisoners hardly at all as individuals, but rather as personifications, stripped to anonymous skeletons, though each with a slightly differentiated mask, of Hunger. In medieval drama, Everyman could be analysed in terms of the personified constituent qualities of the human make-up, and his internal conflict presented in terms of their clash – Love, Anger, Lust, Pity. In the camps it could seem as if, when it came to the crunch, the ultimate, the only essential quality of man was animal hunger; all other qualities were but fatty accretions, inessential and permissible only in certain artificially contrived conditions of civilization; all luxuries, and the idea of a soul a belch, after the rice issue had been unexpectedly large. The memory, and still-live awareness of this standard of value, is often frightening but also exhilarating, and I am unable for long to take much for granted. For example, some time back, there was a little crisis over a party.

I do not go willingly to parties. I have difficulty enough in normal circumstances in communication, and the barriers against communication that parties set up seem gratuitous and unnecessary inflictions. To manage parties you need to be either well advanced in strident neuroticism or a fully integrated personality. Neurotic I may be, but not strident; I can make no claim to an integrated personality. One knows about those who can, filling up their skin with complete, detailed efficiency like a very well-packed suitcase. They are enviable, and recognizable; they are all there. The description, once much in use, of someone being 'not quite all there' seems less common now, no doubt because the science of psychology has analysed the state of being not quite all there into various divisions and subdivisions, each with its specific technical label; he's schizoid, they say, or paranoiac, or whatever. In an old-fashioned stubbornness I am happier to cling to the proposition that I am not quite all there; I mean I have a very tenuous personality. As I have indicated, I do not think this is entirely a bad thing, to be spread about a bit, but it does cause difficulties, particularly at parties, where you tend to find yourself playing a succession of characters like a quick-change actor. The party I have in mind – I had felt obliged to go because it was for the publication of a book by someone I admire very much – was packed with strident neurotics and fully integrated personalities in full boom. Against this I could set the fact that there were many very good pictures on the walls and many men actively pursuing the guests with bottles, urging them to drink. I talked to a great many people, and with each new person I had to reach out into the smoke and grab me down a new and always incomplete personality; now I was an art critic, now I was the husband of my wife, now I was an official. Then a novelist, an art historian, a famous painter who has the same surname as myself, and then unexpectedly an *aficionado* of the bullfight. Then I washed up against my host, at least I think he must have been the host, and we looked at each other face to face very close for thirty seconds without saying anything at all, before he turned away. I was indeed by then drained of any personality at all, dizzy; it was time to go, but as I was going a man I had been listening to earlier touched me on the sleeve and said: 'Excuse me – such a stupid question – but who, exactly, are you?'

A few minutes later I was in the Underground, going home, reading my invitation card; it was quite in order, it named my name, and I had honoured it, but still that last question boomed away in my head. It was the witching hour in the London Underground. There is that time in the evening, not long after the rush hour, when nobody travels in the Tube except expended newspapers, empty cigarette boxes and very sparse foreigners, and, sometimes, me. There was a fairly large party of French at the far end, all apparently drunk, but no one at all at my end, and I was free to sit in the rackety train, boring its way through the subterranean dark, and to think of the most awful ghost story I had ever heard because I could not not think of it.

It is a true story, told me by a friend who was once an alien, and who got swept up with all the other aliens into internment when the great invasion panic of 1940 was on in England. After long weeks,.entirely cut off from kith and kin, they ended up behind barbed wire in a camp on the Isle of Man; there, after a while, they were allowed to make limited contact with the world outside. My friend, though a German alien, was bilingual in English also, and so was given the job of acting as kind of Post Office sorter. One of his fellow internees was not unusual in his circumstances; that is, he had been busy escaping from one place to another across Europe for years, gradually shedding all possessions in his flight. Now about all he had left was his wife, but the 1940 panic had separated the sexes, and so he had nothing. Naturally, therefore, as soon as channels of communication were reopened, he shafted a telegram very urgently out of his barbed wire into the outside world, to his wife. They were only allowed a minimum of words; his message had to be short. Eventually the answer came back from his wife, who, he had thought, was the only living, knowing and loving thing left in the world for him. My friend saw it as it went through his clearing office. It was short too. It said: I AM WELL, WHO ARE YOU.

Just a typist's slip, of course, or a decoding error; those three letters H, O, W, got in the wrong order. Or did they? The doubt remains, and I sat in the train in doubt while hundreds of people got on at Earls Court. Then, at Hammersmith, which is my home station, most of them got off again, including me. I came round the corner on to the towpath at the riverbank and along to my house and there it was, still standing, wife, children, everything.

Within time, through the gradual thriftless spending of season upon season, my wife, our children, form my only constant though ever changing terms of reference. Without them, the mirror would be empty. Recently, as the older children threatened take-off, and while there was still time, we got another child, a calculated folly, a slap in the face of middle age. Drooling over it, I see my bright and eager and witty father softening into senility, incontinence and death. The child, lifted, stamps on my chest like any grave – then laughs, with the fearless, divine and confident ignorance of the five month old, and hands me off with a great male fist like a footballer's.

Excellent to know one is worthless, and alive.

David Piper

The Human Condition

In this motel where I was told to wait,
The television screen is stood before
The picture window. Nothing could be more
Use to a man than knowing where he's at,
And I don't know, but pace the day in doubt
Between my looking in and looking out.

Through snow, along the snowy road, cars pass
Going both ways, and pass behind the screen
Where heads of heroes sometimes can be seen
And sometimes cars, that speed across the glass.
Once I saw world and thought exactly meet,
But only in a picture by Magritte,

A picture of a picture, by Magritte,
Wherein a landscape on an easel stands
Before a window opening on a land-
scape, and the pair of them a perfect fit,
Silent and mad. You know right off, the room
Before that scene was always an empty room.

And that is now the room in which I stand
Waiting, or walk, and sometimes try to sleep.
The day falls into darkness while I keep
The TV going; headlights blaze behind
Its legendary traffic, love and hate,
In this motel where I was told to wait.

Howard Nemerov

Human Condition

Now it is fog, I walk
Contained within my coat;
No castle more cut off
By reason of its moat:
Only the sentry's cough,
The mercenaries' talk.

The street lamps, visible,
Drop no light on the ground,
But press beams painfully
In a yard of fog around.
I am condemned to be
An individual.

In the established border
There balances a mere
Pinpoint of consciousness.
I stay, or start from, here:
No fog makes more or less
The neighbouring disorder.

Particular, I must
Find out the limitation
Of mind and universe,
To pick thought and sensation
And turn to my own use
Disordered hate or lust.

I seek, to break, my span.
I am my one touchstone.
This is a test more hard
Than any ever known.
And thus I keep my guard
On that which makes me man.

Much is unknowable.
No problem shall be faced
Until the problem is;
I, born to fog, to waste,
Walk through hypothesis,
An individual.

Thom Gunn

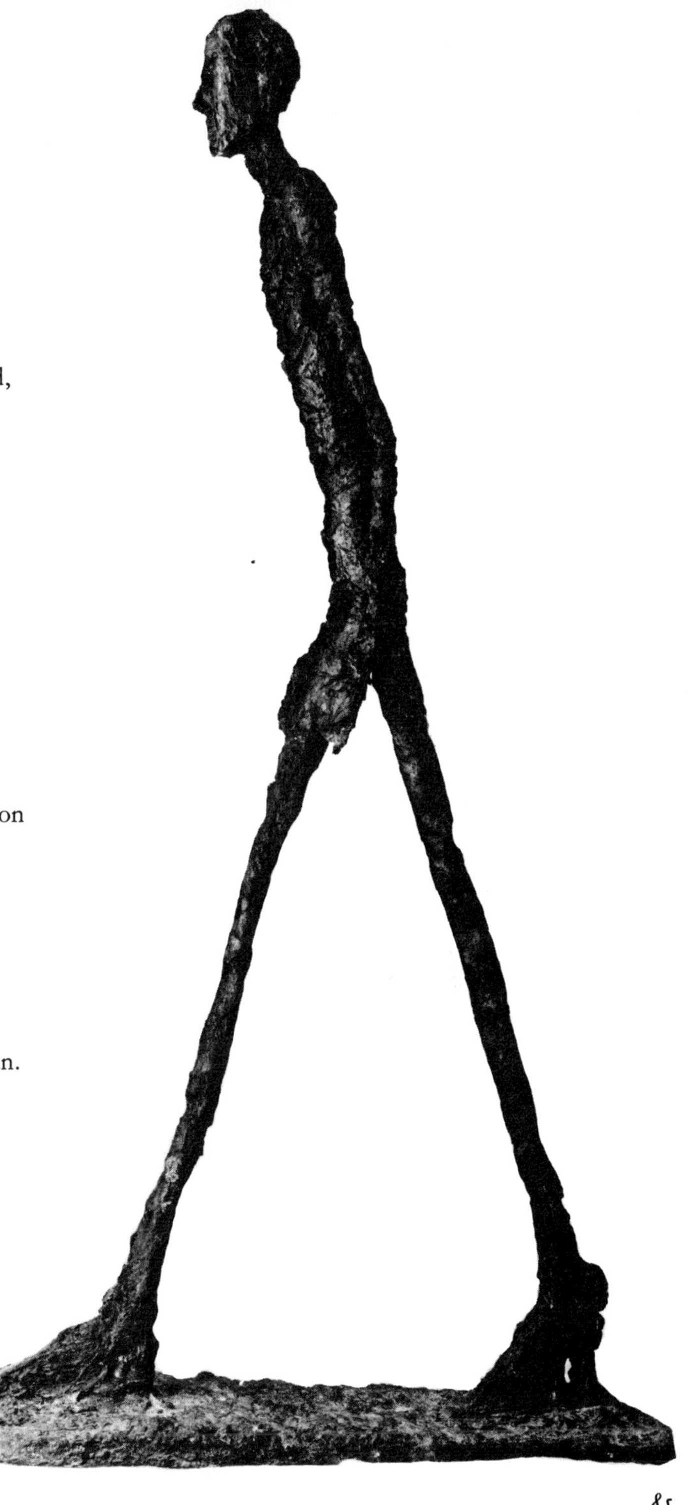

I am

I am – yet what I am, none cares or knows;
   My friends forsake me like a memory lost:
I am the self-consumer of my woes –
   They rise and vanish in oblivious host,
Like shadows in love frenzied stifled throes
   And yet I am, and live – like vapours tost

Into the nothingness of scorn and noise,
   Into the living sea of waking dreams,
Where there is neither sense of life or joys,
   But the vast shipwreck of my lifes esteems;
Even the dearest that I love the best
   Are strange – nay, rather, stranger than the rest.

I long for scenes where man hath never trod
   A place where woman never smiled or wept
There to abide with my Creator God,
   And sleep as I in childhood sweetly slept,
Untroubling and untroubled where I lie
   The grass below, above, the vaulted sky.

John Clare

Departure's Girl Friend

Loneliness leapt in the mirrors, but all week
I kept them covered like cages. Then I thought
Of a better thing.

And though it was late night in the city
There I was on my way
To my boat, feeling good to be going, hugging
This big wreath with the words like real
Silver: *Bon Voyage*.

The night
Was mine, but everyone's, like a birthday.
Its fur touched my face in passing. I was going
Down to my boat, my boat,
To see it off, and glad at the thought.
Some leaves of the wreath were holding my hands
And the rest waved good-bye as I walked, as though
They were still alive.

And all went well till I came to the wharf, and no one.

I say no one, but I mean
There was this young man, maybe
Out of the merchant marine,
In some uniform, and I knew who he was; just the same
When he said to me where do you think you're going,
I was happy to tell him.

But he said to me, it isn't your boat,
You don't have one. I said, it's mine, I can prove it:
Look at this wreath, I'm carrying to it,
Bon Voyage. He said, This is the stone wharf, lady,
You don't own anything here.

And as I
Was turning away, the injustice of it
Lit up the buildings, and there I was
In the other and hated city
Where I was born, where nothing is moored, where
The lights crawl over the stone like flies, spelling now,
Now, and the same fat chances roll
Their many eyes; and I step once more
Through a hoop of tears and walk on, holding this
Buoy of flowers in front of my beauty,
Wishing myself the good voyage.

W. S. Merwin

A Ten-Day Voyage

Jesse Watkins is now a well-known sculptor. I am glad to know him as a friend.

He was born 31 December 1899. Went to sea in 1916 on a tramp steamer during the First World War. His first trip was to North Russia. In the same year he was torpedoed in the Mediterranean. In 1932 he served in a square-rigged sailing ship.

He ended the Second World War (during which he served in the Royal Navy) as a Commander and Commodore of coastal convoys. During his career at sea he encountered shipwreck, mutiny and murder.

He has drawn and painted since early youth and constantly did so at sea. While ashore for brief periods he attended sporadically life classes at Goldsmiths' College and Chelsea Art School. He has also written and had published short stories of the sea.

Twenty-seven years ago Watkins went through a 'psychotic episode' that lasted ten days. I tape-recorded a discussion with him about it in 1964 and with his permission extracts are presented here.

The material speaks for itself. It is an account of his voyage into inner space and time. Its general features are not unusual, but it is unusual to have such a lucid account of them. Although the events are twenty-seven years old, they are vivid in his mind and constitute one of the most significant experiences of his life.

The preliminaries

Before his voyage began, Jesse had 'moved into an entirely new environment'. He had been working seven days a week, until late at night. He felt physically, emotionally, spiritually at a 'low ebb'. Since it is the voyage itself that we are concerned with here, we shall not go into the antecedent circumstances in more detail. Then he was bitten by a dog, and the wound did not heal. He went to hospital where he was given a general anaesthetic for the first time in his life and had the wound dressed.

He returned home by bus and sat down in a chair. His son aged seven came into the room and Jesse saw him in a new and strange way, somehow unremoved from himself.

Then it began.

The voyage

'. . . suddenly I looked at the clock and the wireless was on and then the music was playing – um – oh, popular sort of bit of music. It was based on the rhythm of a tram. Taa-ta-ta-taa-taa – something like Ravel's repetitive tune. And then when that happened I suddenly felt as if time was going back. I felt this time going back, I had this

extraordinary feeling of – er – that was the greatest feeling I had at that moment was of time going backwards. . . .

'I even felt it so strong I looked at the clock and in some way I felt that the clock was reinforcing my own opinion of time going back although I couldn't see the hands moving – – – I felt alarmed because I suddenly felt as if I was moving somewhere on a kind of conveyor belt – and unable to do anything about it, as if I was slipping along and sliding down a – shute as it were and – er – unable to stop myself. And – um – this gave me a rather panicky feeling – I remember going into the other room in order to see where I was, to look at my own face, and there were no mirrors in that room. I went into the other room, and I looked into a mirror at myself, and I looked in a way strange, I seemed as though I were looking at someone who – someone who was familiar but – er – very strange and different from myself – as I felt – – and then I had extraordinary feelings that I was quite capable of doing anything myself, that I had a feeling of being in control of – of all my faculties, body and everything else, – – and I started rambling on.'

One sees the old and familiar in a new and strange way. Often as though for the first time. One's old moorings are lost. One goes back in time. One is embarked on the oldest voyage in the world.

'My wife became very – um – worried. She came in and told me to sit down and lie down in bed and because she was alarmed she got hold of the man next door to come in. He was a civil servant and he was also a bit alarmed and he calmed me down, and I was rambling on to him, and the doctor came up – um – and I was talking of a lot of these feelings I had in my mind about time going back. Of course, to me they sounded perfectly rational, I was going back and thinking that I was going back into sort of previous existences, but only vaguely. And they obviously looked at me as if I were mad, I could feel – I could see the look in their faces and I felt it was not much good talking to them because they obviously thought I was quite round the bend, as I might have been. And – um – then the next thing was that an ambulance came and I was taken off. . . .'

He was taken to an observation ward.

'I was put into bed and – um – – well, I remember that night it was an appalling sort of experience because I had the – had the feeling that – um – that I was then – that I had died. And felt that other people were in beds around me, and I thought they were all other people that had died – and they were there – just waiting to pass on to the next department . . .'

He had not died physically, but his 'ego' had died. Along with this ego-loss, this death, came feelings of the enhanced significance and relevance of everything. . . .

'. . . then I started going into this – – real feeling of regression in time. I had quite extraordinary feelings of – living, not only *living*, but – er – feeling and – er – experiencing everything relating to something I felt that was – well, something like animal life and so on. At one time I actually seemed to be wandering in a kind of landscape with – um – desert landscape – as if I were an animal, rather – rather a large animal. It sounds absurd to say so but I felt as if I were a kind of rhinoceros or something like that and emitting sounds like a rhinoceros and being at the same time afraid and at the same time being aggressive and on guard. And then – um – going back to further periods of regression and even sort of when I was just struggling like something that had no brain at all and as if I were just struggling for my own existence against other things which were opposing me. And – um – then at times I felt as if I were like a baby – I could even – I – I could even hear myself cry like a child. . . .

'All these feelings were very acute and – um – real and, and at the same time I was – I had – I was aware of them, you know, I've got the memory of them still. I was aware of these things happening to me – in some vague sort of way, I was a sort of observer of myself but yet experiencing it. I had all kinds of feelings of – this sounds, because it's nearly thirty years since I experienced it, it sounds a bit disjointed because I've got to drag it out of my memory but I want to be particular that I'm only telling exactly what happened to me and not embellishing it with any sort of imagination or anything like that. Um – I found that I had periods when I came right out of this state, that I'd been sort of moving into, and then comparatively lucid states I had, but I was reading – I read newspapers, because they gave me newspapers and things to read, but I couldn't read them because everything that I read had a large number of associations with it. I mean I'd just read a headline and the headline of this item of news would have – have quite sort of – very much wider associations in my mind. It seemed to start off everything I read and everything that sort of caught my attention seemed to start off bang-bang-bang, like that, with an enormous number of associations moving off into things so that it became so difficult for me to deal with that I couldn't read. Everything seemed to have a much greater – very much greater significance than normally. I had a letter from my wife. I remember the letter she wrote to me and she said, 'The sun is shining here' – and – er – 'It's a nice day.' This is one of the phrases in the letter. There were a number of other phrases and I can't remember all of them and I can't remember all of the phrases in the letter which evoked responses in me, but I remember this one. She said 'The sun is shining here.' And I felt that if it were – that this was a letter from *her*, she was in a quite different world. She was in a world that I could never inhabit any more – and this gave me feelings of alarm and I felt somehow that I was – I'd gone off into a world that I could never move out of.'

Although out of the safe harbour of one's own identity anchored in this time and this place, the traveller may still be clearly aware of this time and place *as well*.

'You know, I was perfectly well aware of myself and aware of the surroundings.'

He had a 'particularly acute feeling' that things were divided into three levels: an antechamber level, a central world and a higher world. Most people were waiting in the antechamber to get into the next department, which was what he had now entered:

'. . . they were sort of awakening. I was also aware of a – um – a higher sphere, as it were. I mean, I'm rather chary of using some of these phrases because they're used so many times – you know, people talk about spheres and all that sort of thing, but – er – the only thing that I felt – and when I'm describing these things I'm describing more feelings – er – a deeper experience than just looking at the thing . . . an awareness of – um – of another sphere, another layer of existence lying above the – not only the antechamber but the present – lying above the two of them, a sort of three-layered – um – existence. . . .'

'What was the lowest one?'

'The lowest one was just a kind of waiting – like a waiting room.'

'I had feelings of – er – of gods, not only God but gods as it were, of beings which are far above us capable of – er – dealing with the situation that I was incapable of dealing with, that were in charge and were running things and – um – at the end of it, everybody had to take on the job at the top. And it was this business that made it such a devastating thing to contemplate, that at some period in the existence of – er – of oneself one had to take on this job, even for only a momentary period, because you had arrived then at awareness of everything. What was beyond that I don't know. At the time I felt that – um – that God himself was a madman . . . because he's got this enormous load of having to be aware and governing and running things – um – and that all of us had to come up and finally get to the point where we had to experience that ourselves. . . . I know that sounds completely crazy to you but that's what I sort of felt at the time.'

'You mean a "madman" in the sense that people in the state that you were in are taken to be mad?'

'Yes, that's what I meant, that he was – er – he was mad. Everything below him or everything below that got to the point where he got – er – had to treat him like that because he was the one that was taking it all at that moment – and that the – er – the journey is there and every single one of us has got to go through it, and – um – everything – you can't dodge it . . . the purpose of everything and the whole of existence is – er – to equip you to take another step, and another step, and so on. . . .'

Jesse felt that this experience was a stage that everyone would have to go through one way or another in order to reach a higher stage of evolution.

'. . . it's an experience that – um – we have at some stage to go through, but that was only one – and that – many more – a fantastic number of – um – things have got to impinge upon us until we gradually build ourselves up into an acceptance of reality, and a greater and greater acceptance of reality and what really exists – and that any dodging of it could only – delays the time and it's just as if you were going to sea in a boat that was not really capable of dealing with the storms that can rise.'

Eventually he felt he couldn't 'take' any more. He *decided* to come back.

'The nurse told me that sometimes I kept them awake at night by talking. And they – they put me into a padded cell and I said, "Well, don't put me in here," I said, you know, I said, "I can't bear it." But they said, "But you – we've got to try to do it because you make such a noise you know – talking." So they put me into this place and I said, "Well, leave the door open", so they left the door open, and I remember going through that night struggling with – with something that wanted to – some sort of – curiosity or willingness to open myself to – um – experiencing – this, and the panic and the insufficiency of spirit that would enable me to experience it. And during that time I went through – I went through the Stations of the Cross, although I'd never been what you might call a really religious person – I'm not now – and I went through all that sort of – those sort of feelings. Well the – all this experience became – went on for quite a time and I began to – they kept on giving me sedatives to make me sleep, and I – one morning I decided that I was not going to take any more sedatives, and that I had got to stop this business going on because I couldn't cope with it any more. . . .'

The return

'I sat on the bed, and I thought, well, somewhere or other I've got to sort of join up with my present – er – self, very strongly. So I sat on the bed, I clenched my hands together tightly. And the nurse had just been along and said to me, "Well, I want you to take this," and I said, "I'm not taking any more because I should – the more I take of that the less capable I am of doing anything now – I mean – as I said, I shall go under." And so I sat on the bed and I held my hands together, and as – I suppose in a clumsy way of linking myself up with my present self, I kept on saying my own name over and over again and all of a sudden, just like that – I suddenly realized that it was all over. All the experiences were finished, and it was a dramatic – a dramatic ending to it all. And there was a doctor there who had been a naval – a rear admiral surgeon – surgeon rear admiral, and he and I had become friendly because we talked about the sea from time to time. And this nurse came along and said, "You haven't drunk that," and I said, "I told you I'm not drinking it," and he said, "Well, I'll have to go and get the doctor," and I said, "Well you get the doctor." Then the doctor came along and I said, "I don't want any more of that sedative," I said, "I'm quite capable of – of running things normally now," I said, "I'm all right." And he looked at me and he looked at my eyes and he said, "Oh," he said, "I can see that." And he laughed, and that's what happened, and from that moment I had – never had any more of these feelings. . . .'

R. D. Laing *The Politics of Experience*

Billy Talking

Hypomania is a mild manic-depressive psychosis, involving acceleration and extension of thought, flight of ideas, pressure of talk and apparent inexhaustibility. Unprompted or unchecked, Billy could speak for forty minutes without once altering the quiet tone of his voice or the reasonableness of his manner.

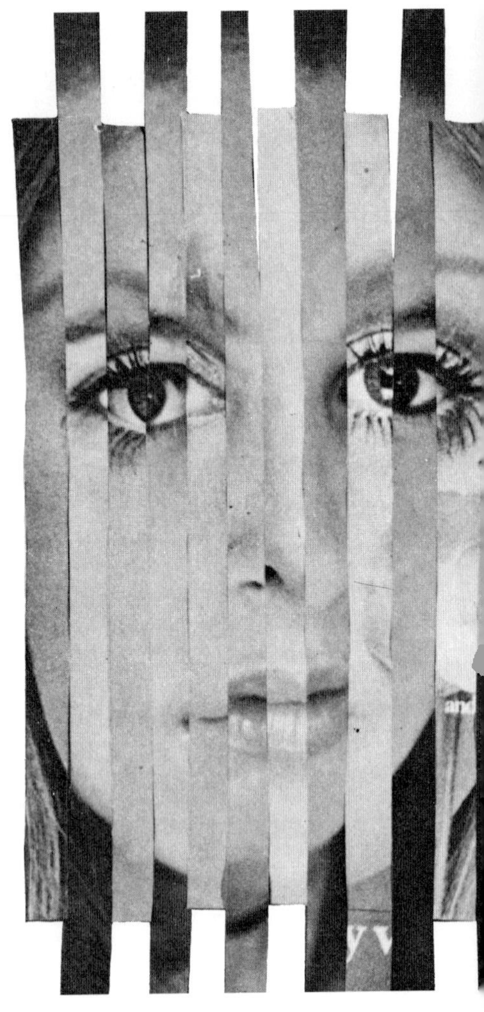

I would say I like political books myself, sir, something of that nature. Herr Hitler's autobiography for instance, I think that's a very good book for someone who takes an interest in political things. It was written from what you might call the patriotic German point of view, putting everything first for Germany. Then there is Mussolini's autobiography which is also a very good book, though in that case it's from an Italian point of view. Hitler being a dark-featured man, you might have thought he would have been a friend of France; but that was not so, nor in Göring's case either though he was more like Mussolini to look at. In fact he could well have been Mussolini's brother, but I don't think he was. And then there was Stalin who was a great supporter of the trades unions, being a communist, although Hitler himself I think would have claimed that what he preached was a form of socialism though he called it 'national socialism', being of a more moderate kind. To my way of looking at it he could certainly be classed as moderately socialist, and that would suit him as a dark-featured person and would mean he could be born in October or December and would take a belief in wood as a study. For instance carpentry would appeal to him: he could take rubber, but I rather doubt that because I think you'd find that Göring was rubber and they would join forces so you'd have wood and rubber together. Mussolini was also dark-featured in a way, and he would have an admiration for June and December and would tend to favour the French who were also dark-featured although they favour May, June and July. On the whole dark-featured people prefer May, June, July, October and December, while fair-haired people favour January, February, August, September and November. The Chinese celebrate June and December and also the first of January, and would be inclined towards friendship with Italy, you see, because they would go to rubber first rather than to wood. That would make sense then because December is a wood month but January is rubber.

I think you'll find August is rubber but with some wood, and June is a wood month, well wood and grass; July would be grass the same as May because July is the son of May or June, whereas June in turn is the son of December. And April, well April is a funny month isn't it, because it's closer to summer than winter? You get January, February, March, which is mostly winter; and April can be inclined to cold but it's heading towards summer. I could be wrong but I think you'd find that April is rubber – because May would definitely be grass and June would be wood. January is rubber and February is wood and rubber, and March is rubber: then April is rubber but springing to wood, which is very funny. May goes to grass with a bit of wood and rubber, and June is wood and grass, followed by July which is all grass. You have say a field or a park in July, so that would be grass wouldn't it? And August. I'm only guessing, but I think it would take rubber, and then in September you'd have rubber leaning to wood. October is definitely wood, I doubt if you'd find it was rubber at all; then November is rubber and December is wood. Yes, that makes sense doesn't it, it definitely saves confusion you see, and apart from April which to my mind is a funny month you get it all sorted out and it gives you much more confidence; well in my case it does, and so I take a great interest in politics. Other people take religion as something to look forward to, or then again others take crime, such as dance-halls or slot-machines, where a good living can be made often only as a result of violence.

To me politics is knowledge really, and if you take a belief in something like that it helps you over your nervousness, or a couple of Aspros and a glass of milk can make you feel much more steady about it. In this sense nature is insoluble and so politics helps.

Like sightless fish in a black cavern, trapped in a sunless ravine uncharted beneath some deep and lonely distant sea, his thoughts flounder endlessly, churning through mud-choked eddies of swirling words. Once there was daylight, love and childhood, with his father strong, lifting an anchor and letting him have a try at steering his barge, and a mother who comforted him under a fearful sky. But that was a long time ago; now for this man there is only jumping from doorways in the dark, searching through garbage, wandering, prison, decrepitude and age.

Tony Parker *The Twisting Lane*

6me SAISON RUSSE

Diary Entries

She tells my wife stupid things in Spanish and I understand Spanish. Spanish is a simple language and is therefore easily understood by a man with feeling. To understand does not mean to know all the words. I understand in every language. I know few words but my sense is keenly developed. I like developing my sense, because I must understand everything that is being said.

I will pretend to be dying, or ill, in order to enter the cottage of the poor. I smell out the poor like a dog scenting out game. I smell very well. I will find the poor without their advertisements. I need no advertisements. I will go by scent. I will not be mistaken. I will not give money to the poor, I will give them life. Life is not poverty. Poverty is not life. I want life. I want love.

I feel that my wife is afraid of me because her movements were determined when I asked her to give me some ink. She felt cold and I too. I am afraid of the cold because it is death. I will write quickly because I am not given much time. I would very much like Kostrovsky* to help me because he understands me. I would speak and he would write and in this way we could do something else as well. I can write and think of something else. I am God in man. I feel what Christ felt. I am like Buddha. I am the Buddhist God and every kind of God. I know each of them. I have met them all. I pretend to be mad on purpose, for my own aims. I know that if everyone thinks that I am a harmless madman they will not be afraid of me. I do not like people who think that I am a dangerous lunatic. I am a madman who loves mankind. *My madness is my love towards mankind.*

I told my wife that I had invented a fountain-pen which will make us a lot of money, but she does not believe me because she thinks that I do not understand what I am doing. I showed her the pen and a pencil, to explain my invention. I will send it to Steinhardt, my lawyer and friend, and will ask him to patent it. Steinhardt is a clever man and will therefore understand the importance of my invention. I want to sell my patent. If they will agree, I will sell it. If they don't, I will destroy it.

I am not rich and do not want riches. I want love and therefore want to throw aside all sordid money – dirt. I will give life to the poor. They will not die of hunger. I won't starve either because I know what to do in order to prevent this.

I am not a child prodigy to be exhibited – I am a sensible man. Millions of years have gone by since the creation of man. Men think that God is where technical inventions are most advanced. God was already there when there was no mechanism. Steel is a necessary thing, but it is also a terrible thing. An aeroplane is a terrible thing. I flew in an aeroplane and cried in it. I do not know why, but I felt that aeroplanes destroy birds. All birds fly away at the sight of an aeroplane. An aeroplane is a

*Kostrovsky was Nijinsky's friend, a Tolstoyan, who tried to influence him greatly. He was epileptic and died insane.

useful thing but it must not be exaggerated. It is a thing coming from God and therefore I like it, but it must not be used for the purpose of war. An aeroplane should express goodwill. I like aeroplanes and will therefore fly in them where there are no birds. I love birds. I do not want to frighten them. A well-known flyer was flying in Switzerland and flew into an eagle. The eagle is savage and does not like other birds, but one must not kill him because God gave him life.

I went to two schools in Petersburg, where they taught me enough. I did not need a university education, as it was not necessary for me to know a great deal.

I do not like universities because they spend their time on politics. Politics are death. Politics are invented by the governments. Men have lost their way and cannot understand each other and have therefore divided themselves into parties. I forgot about the aeroplane which hit an eagle. The eagle is a bird of God and one must not kill tsars, emperors and kings. I like tsars and the aristocrats, but their deeds are not always good deeds. I will give them a good example, by not destroying them. I will help them in every way because I love God, but I beg everyone to help me in this, because, alone, I cannot do everything God wants. I want everyone to help me and they must all come to me for help. I am God and my address is in God. I do not live in the streets, I live in men. I want to work on the feelings of men. I love simple feeling which everyone has. I do not want people with bad feelings. . . .

I do not study people's character in order to write about them. I want to write in order to explain to people their habits – which lead them to death. I call this book *Feelings*. I love feeling and will write a big book about it. There will be a description of my life in it. I do not want to publish this book after my death. I want to publish it now. '*I am afraid for you because you are afraid for yourself. I want to say the truth. I do not want to hurt people. Perhaps you will be put in prison for writing this book. I will be with you because you love me. I cannot be silent. I must speak. I know you will not be put in prison; legally you have not committed an offence. If people want to judge you, you shall answer that everything you said is God's word. Then they will put you into an asylum, and you will understand insane people. I want you to be put in a prison or into an asylum. Dostoyevsky went to the gallows and therefore you also can go and sit somewhere. I know people whose love is not dead and they will not allow you to be put anywhere. You will become as free as a bird when this book is published in many thousands of copies. I want to sign the name of Nijinsky – but my name is God. I love Nijinsky not as Narcissus but as God.*' I love him because he gave me life. I do not want to pay any compliments. I love him. He loves me because he knows my habits. '*Nijinsky has faults, but Nijinsky must be listened to because he speaks the words of God.*' I am Nijinsky. '*I do not want Nijinsky to be hurt and therefore I will protect him. I am only afraid for him because he is afraid for himself. I knew his strength. He is a good man. I am a good God. I do not like Nijinsky when he is bad.*' I do not like God when He is bad. I am God,

Nijinsky is God. '*He is a good man and not evil. People have not understood him and will not understand him if they think. If people listened to me for several weeks there would be great results. I hope that my teachings will be understood.*' *All* that I write is necessary to mankind. Romola is afraid of me, she feels I am a preacher. Romola does not want her husband to be a preacher, she wants a young, handsome husband. I am handsome, young. She does not understand my beauty, I have not got regular features. Regular features are not like God. God has sensitiveness in the face, a hunchback can be Godlike. I like hunchbacks and other freaks. I am myself a freak who has feeling and sensitiveness, and I can dance like a hunchback. I am an artist who likes all shapes and all beauty. Beauty is not relative. Beauty is God, He is in beauty and feeling. Beauty is in feeling too. I love beauty. I feel it and understand it. Those people who think write nonsense about beauty. One cannot discuss it. One cannot criticize it. I am feeling beauty. I love beauty.

I do not want evil – I want love. People think that I am an evil man. I am not. I love everybody. I have written the truth. I have spoken the truth. I do not like untruthfulness and want goodness, not evil. I am love. People take me for a scarecrow because I put on a small cross which I liked. I wore it to show that I was Catholic. People thought I was insane. I was not. I wore the cross in order to be noticed by people. People like calm men. I am not. I love life. I want it. I do not like death. I want to love mankind. I want people to believe in me. I have said the truth about A., Diaghilev and myself. I do not want war and murders. I want people to understand me. I told my wife that I would destroy the man who would touch my notebooks, but I will cry if I have to do it. I am not a murderer. I know that everyone dislikes me. They think I am ill. I am not. I am a man with intelligence.

The maid came and stood near me, thinking that I was sick. I am not. I am healthy. I am afraid for myself because I know God's wish. God wants my wife to leave me. I do not want it, I love her and will pray that she may remain with me. They are telephoning about something. I believe they want to send me to prison. I am weeping, as I love life, but I am not afraid of prison. I will live there. I have explained everything to my wife. She is no longer afraid, but she still has a nasty feeling. I spoke harshly because I wanted to see tears – but not those which have been caused by grief. Therefore I will go and kiss her. I want to kiss her to show her my love. I love her, I want her love. A. has felt that I love her too and she is remaining with us. She is not leaving. She has telephoned to sell her ticket. I do not know for certain but I feel it.

My little girl is singing: 'Ah, ah, ah, ah!' I do not understand its meaning, but I feel what she wants to say. She wants to say that everything – Ah! Ah! – is not horror but joy.

Vaslav Nijinsky *The Diary of Vaslav Nijinsky*

Anxietal Register

DIRECTIONS

Read carefully. Before answering any of the questions below, be sure to have all pages of this form, in order. Fill out in triplicate, using ballpoint pen or, preferably, indelible pencil. Press hard. **Please print**. Sign name to all copies.

1. State full name at present: ______
2. Full name at birth, or baptism: ______
3. Give *any* aliases, abbreviations *or nicknames* by which you have ever been known: ______
4. Attach copies of birth and baptismal certificates.
5. Social security number: ______
6. Name on your last income-tax return: ______
7. Date: ______
8. Date of tax return: ______
9. State your full permanent address: ______
10. Where may you be quickly reached by: ______
    (a) Mail: ______
    (b) Telephone: ______
    (c) Telegram or cable: ______
    (d) Messenger: ______
11. List every address at which you have resided, since birth, in chronological order. Include *every* address, with the following exceptions:
    (a) Hotel accommodations in the United States, Mexico or Canada, for stays of up to or less than three days, occurring more than five years ago.
    (b) Accommodation at US Embassies, in other than an official capacity, for any duration, occurring more than seventeen years ago.
    (c) Antarctic expeditions not using APO addresses.
    All other addresses must be shown, without exception.
    Note: extra sheets (Form AR-B Supplem.) may be attached.
    Street address: City: State: Date from: Date to:
    ______
12. Occupation: ______
13. Name and address of company where you are presently employed/were last employed: ______
    (a) Last position held: ______
14. Salary: ______
15. Name of superior: ______
16. Starting date: ______
17. Terminating date: ______
18. Attach references.
19. If unemployed, give reason: ______
20. Why did you leave your last job? ______

21. Give your entire employment history, except for your last or present job. List all employment in chronological order, and include part-time employment.
Note: extra sheets (Form AR-B Supplem.) may be attached.
Company name & address: Position: Supervisor: Salary:

From: To: Reason for leaving:

22. Have you ever been fired for:
(a) Theft:
(b) Embezzlement:
(c) Dishonesty:
(d) False References:
(e) Absenteeism:
(f) Tardiness:
(g) Loafing:
(h) Inefficiency:
(i) Personal reasons (Explain):

23. Have you ever quarrelled with fellow employees?

24. Have you ever had difficulty with employers? Describe:

25. Have you ever stolen any property belonging to an employer, no matter how small in value?

26. Have you ever feigned illness?

27. Name of your bank or banks?

28. Explain any foreign bank accounts:

29. Bank Account Number(s):

30. Present balance(s):

31. Number and amount of withdrawals during past year:

32. Father's name:

33. Mother's maiden name:

34. Attach birth certificate and marriage licence.

35. Have you ever been arrested:
(a) As a minor:
(b) As an adult:
(c) Misdemeanor?
(d) Felony?
(e) Convicted?
(f) Sentenced?

36. Give full details of any arrest and/or conviction, including name of offence, whether convicted, sentence and/or fine. Include all traffic offences other than overtime parking.

37. Do you love your mother more than your father?

38. If you do not love your mother, explain:

39. Circle which of the following you have ever suffered from:
(a) Rheumatism (b) Arthritis (c) Chronic fatigue (d) Rupture (e) Tuberculosis (f) Night sweats (g) Nocturnal emissions (h) Nightmares (frequent) (i) Sleepwalking (j) Ringing noises (k) Chronic or severe headaches (l) Bronchitis (m) Homosexual tendencies (n) Hot flushes (o) Tumours (p) Cancer (q) Gastric ulcer (r) Gonorrhea (s) Syphilis (t) Asthma (u) Hay fever (v) Severe cough (w) Trenchmouth (x) Hepatitis (jaundice) (y) Diabetes (z) Anaemia (aa) Poliomyelitis (ab) Heart attack (ac) Stroke (ad) Heart murmur (ae) Blindness (af) Deafness (ag) Tunnel vision (ah) Astigmatism (ai) Unexplainable pains (Explain) (aj) Visions (ak) Epilepsy (al) Impotence (am) Obesity (an) Chronic nausea (ao) Drug addition (Explain) (ap) Alcoholism (aq) Double vision (ar) Frequent or severe accidents (as) Amnesia (at) Laryngitis (au) Malnutrition (av) Precognition (aw) Cleft palate (ax) Harelip (ay) Multiple digits (az) Paralysis (specify).

40. Have you ever had any serious physical or mental disorder?
Describe, specifying dates, physician, treatment, hospitalization, etc.: ____________
____

41. Briefly describe your own condition at present: ____________

42. Are you under medication? Describe: ____________

43. Attach medical records and physician's affidavit.

44. Have you ever undergone surgery? Describe: ____________

45. Have you all your natural teeth? (Attach chart) ____________

46. Describe any amputations, giving dates and reasons: ____________
____

47. Have you:
(a) Both kidneys (b) Both lungs (c) Ovaries (d) Prostate (e) Gall bladder (f) Both eyes (g) A bladder (h) A complete stomach (i) A complete colon (j) Both breasts (k) Lower jaw (l) Nose.

48. Have you ever undergone sterilization? ____________

49. Castration? ____________

50. Hysterectomy? ____________

51. Do you feel sexual desire for, about, during:
(a) Those of your own sex (b) Those of both sexes (c) Children (d) Your mother (e) Your father (f) Your son (g) Your daughter (h) Sister (i) Brother (j) Babies (k) Animals (l) Birds (m) Fish (n) Insects (o) Cripples (p) People who hurt you (q) People whom you hurt (r) People of special professions (describe) (s) People in particular costumes (describe) (t) Watching others in the act of coition (u) Peeping at naked persons (v) Looking at photographs (w) Looking at drawings (x) Drawing pictures (y) Telephoning (z) Confessing sins (aa) Listening to music (ab) Dancing (ac) Exposing one's sex organs to someone else (ad) Rape (ae) All members of the opposite sex, regardless of age or condition (af) Watching movies (ag) Watching television (ah) Performing your ordinary work (ai) Masturbating (aj) Urinating (ak) Defecating (a) Menstruating (am) Wearing clothing belonging to the opposite sex (an) A particular part of another's body (ao) Of your body (ap) Crowds (aq) Rubbing against people (ar) Clergy (as) Weapons (at) Machines (au) Plants (av) Trees (aw) Sunsets (ax) People of other races (ay) Apparel (az) Dangerous or unusual surroundings (ba) Inanimate objects (bb) Mathematical propositions (bc) Thoughts (bd) The Law (be) God (bf) The act of filling out a form.

63. If you are merely reading this form, why do you believe that you have *not* been asked to fill it out? ____________

64. Have you been asked to fill out this form? ____________

65. To read it? ____________

66. Not to fill it out? ____________

67. Not to read it? Explain: ____________

68. Compare this form with others which you may have read or filled out, whether or not you were asked to read them or fill them out: ____________

____

69. Be sure your comparison is fair and correct. If it is not, you may rewrite it on extra sheets (Form AR-B Supplem.). If you do so, be sure your revision is correct.

70. Was your original comparison correct? ____________ Fair? ____________
If not, explain: ____________

71. If you revised your comparison, why? ____________

____

72. Write your life history in brief, explaining in passing your answers to questions 11, 21, 39 and 51 *fully*. Take as much time, and as many extra sheets (Form AR-B Supplem) as necessary, but do *not lie, omit, falsify, distort* or *invent*. If there are any portions you genuinely do not fully remember, you will be asked to complete and attach three copies of Form WH6, Hypnotic Drugs Waiver of Rights. ____________

____

____

____

____

____

73. Sign the following statement:
I hereby agree to submit to a Keeler Polygraph ('Lie Detector') examination, to be conducted by or in the presence of a psychiatrist and police officer, during which I will endeavour to answer all or any questions about my past life as truthfully as I am able.
(X) Signed: ____________
Witnessed: ____________

74. Describe your feelings upon reading and signing the above statement: ____________

____

75. Do you believe you have anything to hide, about your past life? If not, explain: ____________

____

____

____

76. Have you anything to add, regarding the answers to questions 11, 21, 33, 39, 51, 72 or 75? ____________

____

____

____

____

77. Do you ever have feelings of anxiety? ____________

I swear that all the statements above are true and complete and that I have not attempted any falsification, *on penalty of perjury*.
(X) Signed: ____________
Witnessed: ____________

John Sladek *Mind in Chains*

Afternoons

Summer is fading:
The leaves fall in ones and twos
From trees bordering
The new recreation ground.
In the hollows of afternoons
Young mothers assemble
At swing and sandpit
Setting free their children.

Behind them, at intervals,
Stand husbands in skilled trades,
An estateful of washing,
And the albums, lettered
Our Wedding, lying
Near the television:
Before them, the wind
Is ruining their courting-places

That are still courting-places
(But the lovers are all in school),
And their children, so intent on
Finding more unripe acorns,
Expect to be taken home.
Their beauty has thickened.
Something is pushing them
To the side of their own lives.

Philip Larkin

People in a Lift

The everyday banality fascinated me: people enter a lift, an anonymous enclosure which prevents any physical activity for a short space of time.

They stare in front of them, exchange absurd remarks; they are lost in thought, or not at all; they try themselves out in certain roles, or shed them. The same sort of situation, though perhaps less intensive, can be observed in cafés, railway stations or in the tunnel between waiting room and aeroplane. In the cage of the lift there is no chance of escape, and the comparatively short time which one spends there presents no opportunity to engage in any activity.

I chose a lift in a publishing house which accommodates various newspapers and agencies. People there are used to encountering photographers, and the sight of cameras hanging round one's neck is nothing new to them. Even my fingering the shutter release hardly aroused any interest from my neighbours. I used a super-wide-angle lens so that I would not have to raise the camera to eye-level, and acted as if I were completely uninterested in my surroundings. I was thus successful in producing realistic photographs during my five hours and thirty-five minutes in the lift, banal maybe, but informative. The pictures do not aspire to unmask or expose; the dignity of the people photographed remains intact, as I intended.

Heinrich Riebesehl

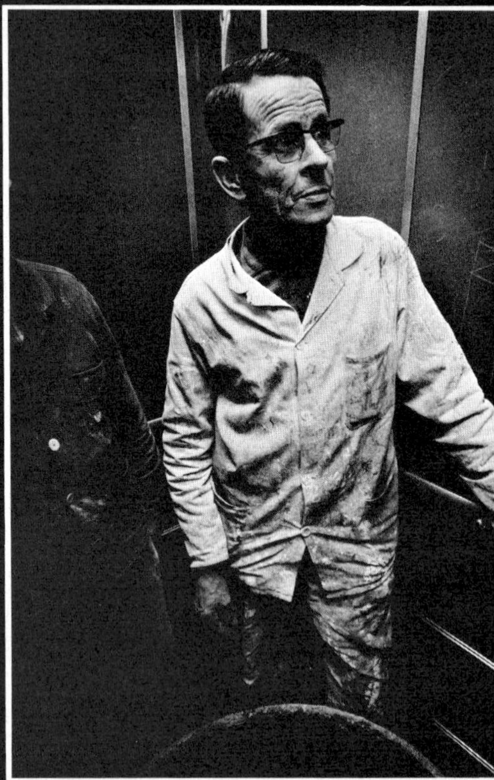

2
K
stern
E

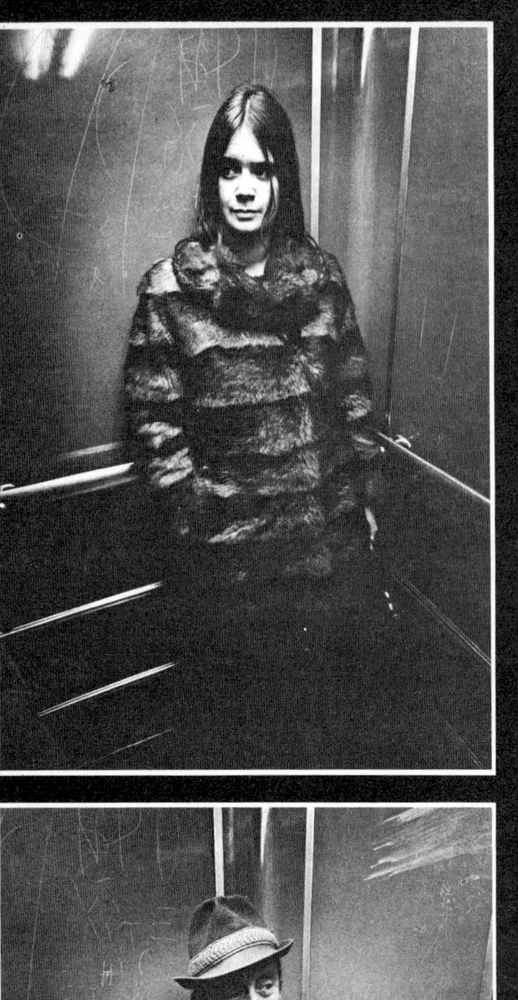

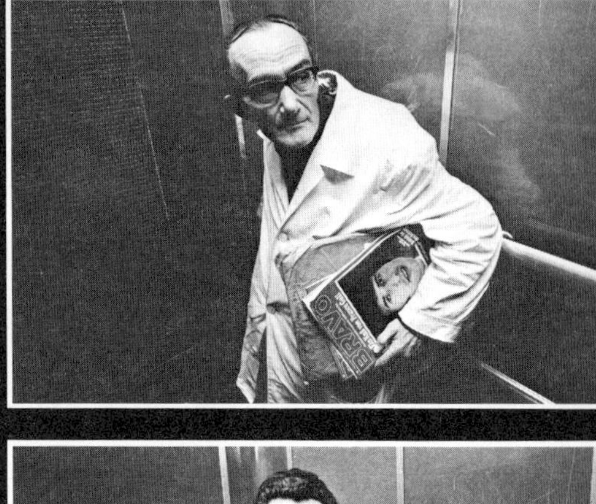
BRAVO

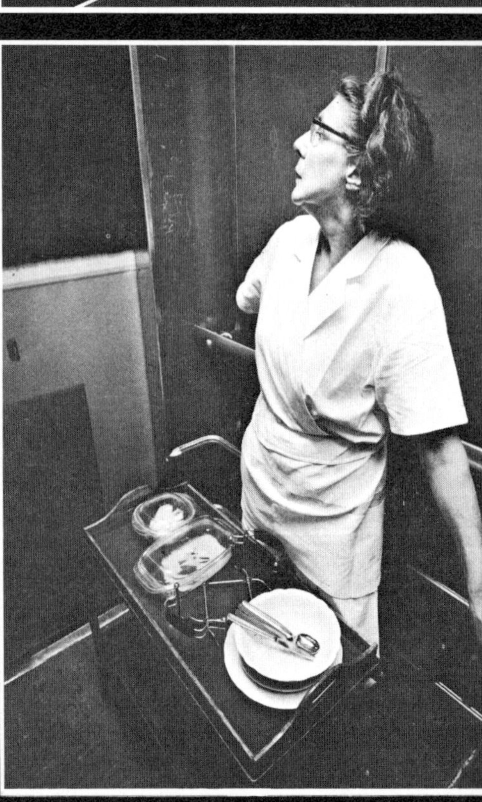

In the Snack-Bar

A cup capsizes along the formica,
slithering with a dull clatter.
A few heads turn in the crowded evening snack-bar.
An old man is trying to get to his feet
from the low round stool fixed to the floor.
Slowly he levers himself up, his hands have no power.
He is up as far as he can get. The dismal hump
looming over him forces his head down.
He stands in his stained beltless gaberdine
like a monstrous animal caught in a tent
in some story. He sways slightly,
the face not seen, bent down
in shadow under his cap.
Even on his feet he is staring at the floor
or would be, if he could see.
I notice now his stick, once-painted white
but scuffed and muddy, hanging from his right arm.
Long blind, hunchback born, half paralysed
he stands
fumbling with the stick
and speaks:
'I want – to go to the – toilet.'

It is down two flights of stairs, but we go.
I take his arm. 'Give me – your arm – it's better,' he says.
Inch by inch we drift towards the stairs.
A few yards of floor are like a landscape
to be negotiated, in the slow setting out
time has almost stopped. I concentrate
my life to his: crunch of split sugar,
slidy puddle from the night's umbrellas,
table edges, people's feet,
hiss of the coffee-machine, voices and laughter,
smell of a cigar, hamburgers, wet coats steaming,
and the slow dangerous inches to the stairs.
I put his right hand on the rail
and take his stick. He clings to me. The stick
is in his left hand, probing the treads.
I guide his arm and tell him the steps.

And slowly we go down. And slowly we go down.
White tiles and mirrors at last. He shambles
uncouth into the clinical gleam.
I set him in position, stand behind him
and wait with his stick.
His brooding reflection darkens the mirror
but the trickle of his water is thin and slow,
an old man's apology for living.
Painful ages to close his trousers and coat –
I do up the last buttons for him.
He asks doubtfully, 'Can I – wash my hands?'
I fill the basin, clasp his soft fingers round the soap.
He washes, feebly, patiently. There is no towel.
I press the pedal of the drier, draw his hands
gently into the roar of the hot air.
But he cannot rub them together,
drags out a handkerchief to finish.
He is glad to leave the contraption, and face the stairs.
He climbs, and steadily enough.
He climbs, we climb. He climbs
with many pauses but with that one
persisting patience of the undefeated
which is the nature of man when all is said.
And slowly we go up. And slowly we go up.
The faltering, unfaltering steps
take him at last to the door,
across that endless, yet not endless waste of floor.
I watch him helped on a bus. It shudders off in the rain.
The conductor bends to hear where he wants to go.

Wherever he could go it would be dark
and yet he must trust men.
Without embarrassment or shame
he must announce his most pitiful needs
in a public place. No one sees his face.
Does he know how frightening he is in his strangeness
under his mountainous coat, his hands like wet leaves
stuck to the half-white stick?
His life depends on many who would evade him.
But he cannot reckon up the chances,
having one thing to do,
to haul his blind hump through these rains of August.
Dear Christ, to be born for this!

Edwin Morgan

The Tea Shop

The girl in the tea shop
                    Is not so beautiful as she was,
The August has worn against her.
She does not get up the stairs so eagerly;
Yes, she also will turn middle-aged,
And the glow of youth that she spread about us
                    As she brought us our muffins
Will be spread about us no longer.
                    She also will turn middle-aged.

Ezra Pound

The Round the World Fliers

Going anywhere near Paterson? he said at the 23rd Street ferry ticket booth. No, I said looking at him closely – red face, mild blue eyes, long chin and sandy hair. Just a kid, more or less. Why? Looking for a ride?

Yeah. Something in the accent, short and sharp. He was bareheaded and coatless in a short-sleeved and narrow-striped blue-and-white sweater shirt. His face sure was sunburned.

O.K. Get in. I drove the car onto the ferry.

Boy! that's a relief, he said. I just walked down from 116th Street and let me tell you those pavements are hot – and hard.

Where are you headed for?

Scranton. I got relatives there.

Been on the road long?

Five days. Am I glad to get out of that city. What kind of a place is that anyway? He shook his head in retrospect.

What's the matter, don't you like it?

My money gave out last night, I haven't had anything to eat since. Think I could get a drink on this boat?

No, I don't think so, this is just for cars – unless you want to ask one of the hands. There must be some place they get water here.

I can wait, he replied. He looked back at the receding shore line and again shook his head slowly from side to side as if in thought. At this moment it came on to rain in a great burst of heavy drops like marbles pelting the low waves into a thousand pits and a greyish mist of spray.

Think this will last?

No, not more than a few minutes, I said.

It'll cool things off anyway. I hope I never see that place again, he returned to his old theme.

Don't blame you, I said. I don't like it either.

You know, he went on, I stopped in at a restaurant around one o'clock this afternoon thinking maybe I could wash dishes or sweep the place out or something for a sandwich and a cup of coffee. It wasn't a fancy place and not a rough joint either, just ordinary. Boy, what a reception *I* got. I've never done any panhandling but I figured I was willing to work for anything I asked for. I almost got thrown out of the place. The man came out from behind the counter at me, I thought he was going to throw me out bodily. I didn't even stop for a drink.

What'll you have? I asked him when the soda-pop man came by.

Cream soda, he said.

Let me have a straw with it, I told the man.

Yes, sir.

Boy, does that taste good! I tell you you get awfully empty when you can't even get water to drink in a place. You can do an awful lot of walking on just water, you'd be surprised how it picks you up. I've often heard it said an army marches on its stomach. Do I know that now!

Where you from?

Montreal.

Out of a job?

I was only working two and three days a week, then I got laid off entirely – for ten days. They told me I might get steady work after that so I thought I'd look around a bit – while I had the chance. I thought I'd take a look at the city first, then head for Scranton. My relatives will get me home if I can't find anything there.

Have a cigarette?

No, not now.

What are you, a Scotsman? You look Scotch to me.

No, English, Powner, doesn't that sound like an English name? Charlie Powner. My mother and father were both born in England, one in Burton and the other in Broton, just outside London, on the Trent. That's English enough too, isn't it?

I'm half English myself. Have any trouble finding rides?

Not much. The worst was in the city. I hopped on the back of a couple of trucks and when they'd put me off I'd look for another. Say, did you see the fliers come over?

No, I replied. I'm just in on a quick trip. Did you see them?

What a racket! Around two o'clock, I guess it was. I had turned into the park so I could set foot on the grass there for a while to rest my feet after those hot pavements. All of a sudden I heard a tremendous noise all around me, factory whistles, taxi horns, people shouting. What the hell is this? I said. I couldn't make it out. Then I hear the roar of the motors and saw the plane overhead.

Only 5¢
PHI

LIES

Was it flying low?

Not so very, but you could tell it by the colour and the two tail fins, the two rudders. What a welcome! It was a regular bedlam in the city for a few minutes. A great flight too. I'm glad they got through. But I was worried during those six silent hours after Fairbanks, Alaska. Boy, those Canadian Northwest wilds are worse than anything they'd find in Siberia. If they came down there, we'd never find them. They'll give them a big parade tomorrow, I guess. It ought to be a sight. Not for me, though. I hope to be in Scranton by that time.

Well, you did what you set out to do anyway. You saw the city. How do you fellows eat when you're on the road that way? That's what always gets me.

Well, when I left Montreal I took a dollar. My wife told me I was crazy but I figured I could make it in five days allowing twenty cents a day for food.

What could you eat for that?

Soup mostly. That fills you up.

Yes, I said, and you salt it well it makes up for what you sweat out on the road.

Yes, then you drink a lot of water and you feel fine.

Throw it in the river, I told him seeing him sit there with the empty bottle in his hand. He looked at it, it was a tall well-made green bottle.

No, he said, the fellow will want it back or they'll charge him for it. Just then the Syrian returned with his smile to collect the empty.

Getting off the boat I was busy with the controls and we said nothing until he saw the half-completed works at the Jersey end of the 42nd Street tubes.

What in hell's that? he said. Boy! he said after my explanation, you do things right down here in the States, don't you? Wonderful roads too. But we don't have the auto accidents you do and no kidnapping either. But our roads are awful muddy.

As we began crossing the meadows, he said, There don't seem to be many footing it down here.

Why, did you see more of them upstate?

The roads were black with them between Albany and Boston, but they were mostly headed in an opposite direction from the way I was going, out towards Buffalo and Rochester and places like that. I saw two girls day before yesterday; I could see them coming for quite a while and I'll be damned if I could tell they were girls the way they were dressed. They stopped me to bum a couple of cigarettes from me and even when they spoke to me I thought at first they were boys, only when I looked hard at them did I realize that they were girls.

What's the idea, I said, disguising yourselves that way? Oh, they said, we get by without so much trouble in these clothes. They had come from Boston and were headed for Elmira where they lived.

That's interesting.

I slept with two girls night before last. In a box car. I think it must have been a private car for race horses, it was so clean. I was looking around the yards for a place to flop in. There was a coloured man there and I asked him if it would be all right if I hopped into that one. Sure go ahead, he said. And you'll find good, clean straw there too. So in I got, it was towards evening and did that straw feel good! Boy, I never slept so well in my life, it was like the finest of soft feathers to me. When I woke up in the morning I reached for a cigarette as I always do, first thing, and lit a match. It was getting light anyhow. And there they were, two girls, with skirts on and everything, sleeping in the opposite corner from me. They were snoring away in good style so I got up and left them.

I've read something about that, I said. I understand the railroad men take pretty good care of them through the country.

Yeah, they get the best everywhere. I understand down through the south-west there's nothing but girls. Not for me though. That's one part of the country I'm going to keep out of.

The rain had stopped by now. Steam was rising from the heated roadway. I'm letting you off here, I said. This is Paterson Avenue. Stay right on it and you'll make Paterson without any trouble. If you have any luck you might even get through to Scranton tonight.

Yeah, I'd like to make it, he said. I don't want to leave my wife up there alone too long. I got a little kid too. You ought to see him. All he wants to do is be outdoors. Put him in a pen and he'll stay there all day playing around. But he don't like to be in the house.

Here, I said, this'll get you some supper and a bunk for the night if you need it.

Thanks a million, he said. Do you mind if I help myself to one of those cigarettes now?

Take the pack.

No, thanks. Just one. And if you're ever in Montreal, stop in and see us. 384 Mount Vernon Avenue. Do it. We'll be delighted to see you. A thousand thanks. So long.

As he was standing there speaking the last words I noticed the material of his trousers, a heavy red-brown woollen stuff of a much better quality than any but the wealthy possess in this country.

William Carlos Williams *The Farmers' Daughters*

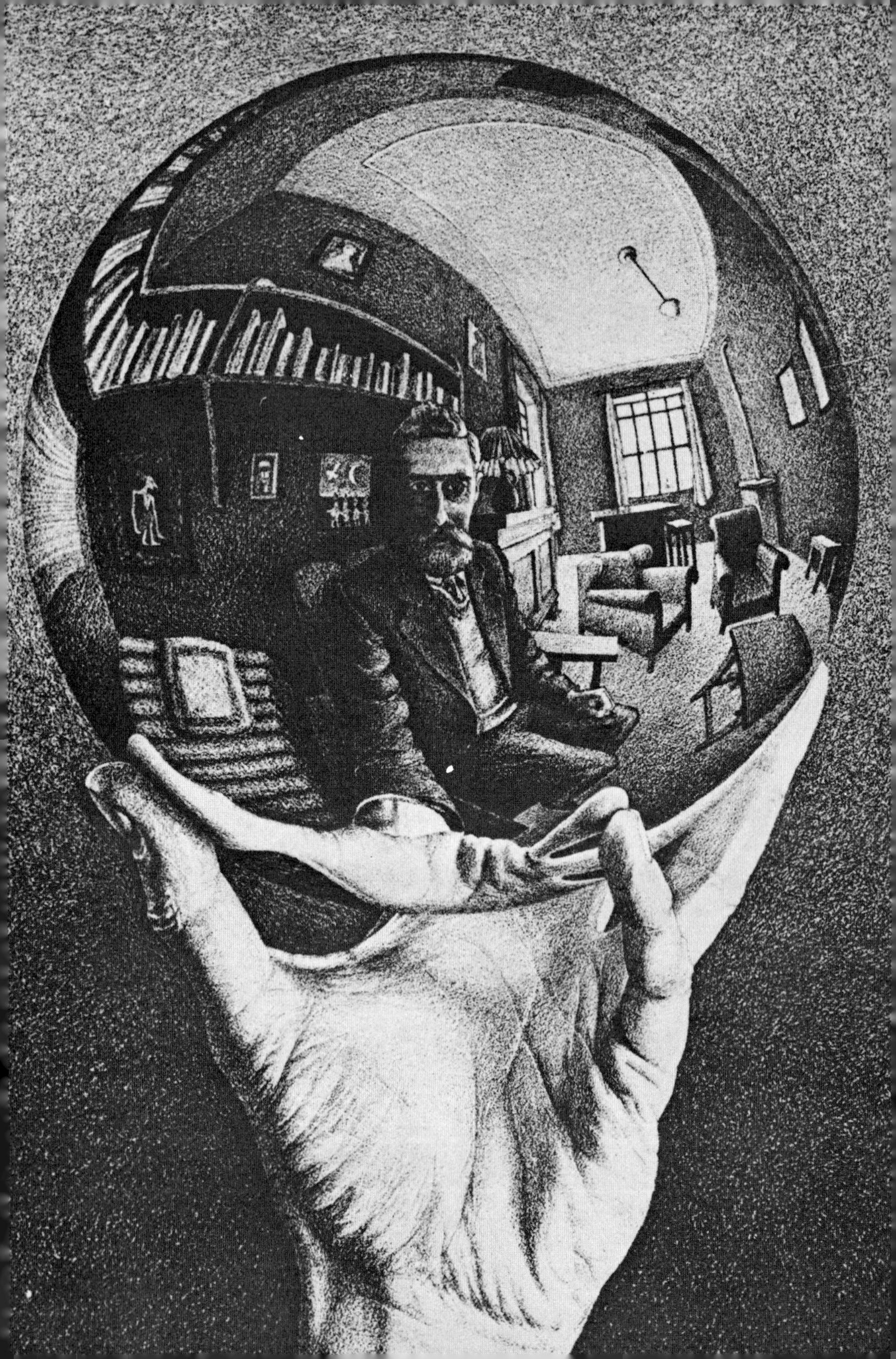

Acknowledgements

For permission to use copyright material acknowledgement is made to the following:

Poems and Prose

For 'The Overloaded Man' by J. G. Ballard to John Farquharson Ltd; for 'Roles' from *Invitation to Sociology: A Humanistic Perspective* by Peter L. Berger to Penguin Books Ltd; for 'Personal Names Tabooed' from *The Golden Bough* by Sir James Frazer to the executors of the estate of the late Sir James Frazer and A. P. Watt & Sons; for 'Human Condition' from *The Sense of Movement* by Thom Gunn to Faber & Faber Ltd; for 'The Soldier in White' from *Catch-22* by Joseph Heller to Jonathan Cape Ltd and the author; for 'The Gigantic Mirror' from *Steppenwolf* by Herman Hesse translated by Basil Creighton and revised by Walter Sorell to Suhrkamp Verlag, Secker & Warburg Ltd and Penguin Books Ltd; for 'Talking to a Stranger' by John Hopkins to Hatton & Bradley Ltd; for 'Stripping Walls' by Brian Jones from *Poems* to London Magazine Editions; for 'Once upon a time' from *Portrait of the Artist as a Young Man* by James Joyce to the executors of the estate of James Joyce and Jonathan Cape Ltd; for 'Growing' by Joseph Korner from *New Pictorial Knowledge* to International Learning Systems Corp. Ltd; for 'Persons, Relations and Families' from *Sanity, Madness and the Family* by R. D. Laing and A. Esterson to Tavistock Publications Ltd; for 'A Ten-Day Voyage' from *The Politics of Experience* by R.D. Laing to Penguin Books Ltd; for 'Afternoons' and 'Reference Back' from *The Whitsun Weddings* by Philip Larkin to Faber & Faber Ltd; for 'Why?' from *The Member of the Wedding* by Carson McCullers to the Cresset Press Ltd and Laurence Pollinger Ltd; for 'Departure's Girl Friend' from *Drunk in the Furnace* by W. S. Merwin to Rupert Hart-Davis Ltd and David Higham Associates Ltd; for 'In the Snack-Bar' from *The Second Life* by Edwin Morgan to Edinburgh University Press; for 'Glass and the Ego' from *Technics and Civilization* by Lewis Mumford to Routledge & Kegan Paul Ltd; for 'The Human Condition' from *The Winter Lighting* by Howard Nemerov to André Deutsch Ltd; for 'Diary Entries' from *The Diary of Vaslav Nijinsky* edited by Romola Nijinsky to Jonathan Cape Ltd and Romola Nijinsky; for 'The Birth of Furriskey' from *At Swim-Two-Birds* by Flann O'Brien to Granada Publishing Ltd; for 'Directions to the Armourer' by Elder Olson to the New Yorker Magazine; for 'Billy Talking' from *The Twisting Lane* by Tony Parker to Anthony Sheil Associates Ltd; for 'The Beast' from *Little Johnny's Confession* by Brian Patten to Allen & Unwin Ltd; for 'Night' from *Landscape and Silence* by Harold Pinter to Methuen & Co. Ltd; for 'I am Well, Who are You' by David Piper from the *Observer* Magazine, 7 July 1968 to A. D. Peters & Co; for 'Mirror' from *Crossing the Water* by Sylvia Plath to Faber & Faber Ltd and Olwyn Hughes Literary Agents; for 'A Hot Bath' from *The Bell Jar* by Sylvia Plath to Faber & Faber Ltd; for 'He has a veranda with a view' from *The Watcher on the Cast Iron Balcony* by Hal Porter to Faber & Faber Ltd; for 'The Tea Shop' from *Collected Shorter Poems* by Ezra Pound to Faber & Faber Ltd; for 'Anxietal Register B' by John Sladek to the author; for 'Modified Man' from *The Biological Time Bomb* by Gordon Rattray Taylor to Thames & Hudson Ltd; for 'Self and Not-Self' from *The Origins of Love and Hate* by Ian D. Suttie to Routledge & Kegan Paul Ltd; for 'The Round the World Fliers' from *The Farmers' Daughters* by William Carlos Williams to New Directions Publishing Corp.; for 'Among School Children' from *The Collected Poems of W. B. Yeats* by W. B. Yeats to Mr M. B. Yeats and the Macmillan Co. Ltd.

Pictures For the picture on pages 8–9 to Marie Castro-Cid; page 11 to Euan Duff; page 12 to Geoffrey Drury; page 14 to C. J. Bucher Ltd; page 17 to the National Library of Australia, Canberra; pages 20–21 to Modinska Knjiga International; page 22 to Walker Evans; page 27 to Paul Oliver; pages 28–9 to Bohomil Stepan; pages 30–31 to Mr and Mrs Robert B. Mayer, Mr and Mrs Jacques Gelman; page 36 to Mr and Mrs James Laughlin; page 39 to the National Museum, Stockholm; pages 40–41 to the National Museum, Stockholm; Staatlich Museum, Berlin; Réunion des Musées Nationaux, Paris; National Gallery of Art, Washington DC; page 42 to the Piccadilly Gallery; pages 48–9 to the Municipal Gallery of Modern Art, Dublin; page 51 to Antonas Sutkas; pages 54–5 to Brighton Museum and Art Gallery; pages 60–61 to the General Electric Company; page 63 to the Museum of Modern Art, New York; pages 64–5 to Paramount; page 68 to John Glashan; page 70 to the Imperial War Museum; page 84 to John Webb; page 85 to Skidmore, Owings & Merrill; page 86 to Northampton Picture Library; pages 88–9 to Jesse Watkins; pages 94–5 to the Marlborough Day Hospital; page 97 to Dr E. Adamson; page 98 to Boris Kochno and Radio Times Hulton Picture Library; pages 106–107 to the Sunday Mirror National Exhibition of Children's Art; pages 108–11 to Heinrich Riebesehl; pages 112–13 to Larry Herman; page 115 to Manchester City Art Galleries; pages 118–19 to the Art Institute of Chicago.

Every effort has been made to trace owners of copyright material, but in some cases this has not proved possible. The publishers would be glad to hear from any further copyright owners of material reproduced in *Identity*.